More Praise for *The Idea-Driven Organization*

"*The Idea-Driven Organization* is an exciting book that makes a compelling case for a simple but very powerful concept—business leaders who learn how to leverage the know-how and ideas of their frontline people will have a major winning edge because most of their competitors either don't get it or don't know how to do it. The detailed and provocative case examples are a major strength of the book—they show how business leaders can put ideas into action by tapping the expertise in their own organization."

—**Lee Bolman, coauthor of *Reframing Organizations***

"We're at the end of the age of being able to do more with less based on tired old management models and thinking. To thrive in the new era, organizations will need to be idea driven. Fortunately, Robinson and Schroeder have written a must-read guide for leaders looking to make this transformation."

—**Chip R. Bell, coauthor of *Managing Knock Your Socks Off Service* and *Managers as Mentors***

"*The Idea-Driven Organization* is a challenge to the dominant paradigm of 'Manager Knows Best,' replacing it with a more balanced program of top-directed but bottom-driven initiative to keep creativity and productivity flowing. It is no less than a call for a complete housecleaning—from physical and spatial relationships, to organization and information flows, and to changing the mindsets of employees and management alike! Required reading in an increasingly globalized and competitive world."

—**Dean Cycon, founder and CEO, Dean's Beans Organic Coffee Company, and winner of a 2013 Oslo Business for Peace Award and the United Nations Women's Empowerment Principles Leadership Award for Community Engagement**

"Robinson and Schroeder have learned from experience the power of people at the front line of the organization actively identifying and solving problems. Building on their previous book, *Ideas Are Free*, they tell us how to create an environment to encourage the free flow of ideas to become a high performing organization."

—**Jeffrey K. Liker, PhD, Professor, University of Michigan, and author of *The Toyota Way***

"To succeed in business today, it is absolutely essential that you tap into the ideas, creativity, and innovation of every member of your team. Working with companies around the world, I have seen that one of the greatest roadblocks to their success is a failure to truly get the most possible value from their talent. I am extremely impressed with this book and have recommended it to many of my clients. The authors lay out a superb blueprint, with lots of tools and examples, for creating an idea-driven organization. This is one of those rare must-read books."

—**John Spence, author of *Awesomely Simple***

The
Idea-Driven
ORGANIZATION

UNLOCKING THE POWER
IN BOTTOM-UP IDEAS

The Idea-Driven ORGANIZATION

Alan G. Robinson
Dean M. Schroeder

Berrett–Koehler Publishers, Inc.
San Francisco
a BK Business book

Berrett-Koehler Publishers, Inc.
235 Montgomery Street, Suite 650
San Francisco, CA 94104-2916
Tel: (415) 288-0260   Fax: (415) 362-2512   www.bkconnection.com

Ordering Information

Quantity sales. Special discounts are available on quantity purchases by corporations, associations, and others. For details, contact the "Special Sales Department" at the Berrett-Koehler address above.

Individual sales. Berrett-Koehler publications are available through most bookstores. They can also be ordered directly from Berrett-Koehler: Tel: (800) 929-2929; Fax: (802) 864-7626; www.bkconnection.com

Orders for college textbook/course adoption use. Please contact Berrett-Koehler: Tel: (800) 929-2929; Fax: (802) 864-7626.

Orders by U.S. trade bookstores and wholesalers. Please contact Ingram Publisher Services, Tel: (800) 509-4887; Fax: (800) 838-1149; E-mail: customer.service@ingrampublisherservices.com; or visit www.ingrampublisherservices.com/Ordering for details about electronic ordering.

Berrett-Koehler and the BK logo are registered trademarks of Berrett-Koehler Publishers, Inc.

Printed in the United States of America

Berrett-Koehler books are printed on long-lasting acid-free paper. When it is available, we choose paper that has been manufactured by environmentally responsible processes. These may include using trees grown in sustainable forests, incorporating recycled paper, minimizing chlorine in bleaching, or recycling the energy produced at the paper mill.

Production Management: **Michael Bass Associates**
Cover Design: Ian Shimkoviak/The Book Designers

Library of Congress Cataloging-in-Publication Data
Robinson, Alan (Alan G.)
    The idea-driven organization : unlocking the power in bottom-up ideas / Alan G. Robinson and Dean M. Schroeder.
        pages   cm
    Includes bibliographical references and index.
    ISBN 978-1-62656-123-6 (hardcover)
    1. Suggestion systems. 2. Management--Employee participation. 3.Organizational change.
4. Organizational effectiveness. 5. Corporate culture. I. Schroeder, Dean M. II. Title.
    HF5549.5.S8R627 2014
    658.4'038—dc23
                                                                    2013050773

First Edition
19 18 17 16 15 14   10 9 8 7 6 5 4 3 2 1

To Margaret, Phoebe,
and Margot

To Kate, Lexie,
Liz, and Tori

CONTENTS

PREFACE

AFTER YEARS OF BEING ASKED to do more with less, managers are increasingly aware that they cannot produce the results that are expected of them with the organizations they currently have and the methods they currently use.

We have now been doing more with less for so long that we have reached a point where further demands can no longer be met by simply tweaking our existing organizations or management methods. Cutting wages, perks, and benefits and pushing people to work harder can go only so far. A different approach is needed. Interestingly, the best solution involves the very people that have been bearing the brunt of the cost so far: ordinary employees.

Every day, front-line employees see many problems and opportunities that their managers do not. They have plenty of ideas to improve productivity and customer service, to offer new or better products or services, or to enhance their organizations in other ways. But their organizations usually do better at suppressing these ideas than promoting them.

In our experience, most managers have difficulty believing that there is enough value in employee ideas to justify the effort of going after them. But as we shall explain, some *80 percent* of an organization's potential for improvement lies in front-line ideas. This fact means that organizations that are not set up to listen to and act on front-line ideas are using at best only a fifth of their improvement engines. And much of their innovation potential is locked up in the same way. When managers gain the ability to implement twenty, fifty, or even a hundred ideas per person per year, *everything changes.*

Today, a growing number of idea-driven organizations have become very good at promoting front-line ideas and as a result are reaching extraordinary levels of performance. Whereas traditional organizations are directed and driven from the top, idea-driven organizations are directed from the top but are *driven by ideas from the bottom.*

A number of years ago, we wrote *Ideas Are Free,* in which we articulated and documented what becomes possible when an organization aggressively pursues front-line ideas. We described companies with the best idea systems in the world and the extraordinary advantages these systems provide. This vision attracted numerous leaders and managers around the world. Some ran with it and were quite successful. But others struggled. We began to get a lot of calls for help.

As we worked alongside managers and leaders trying to implement high-performance idea systems, we learned two important lessons. First, while getting the mechanics of an idea process right is certainly important, to get good results from it often requires significant changes in the way an organization is led, structured, and managed. Second, whereas it is one thing to understand how idea-driven organizations work, it is quite another to know how to create one. These realizations are what led us to write this book.

We began to study the process by which organizations become idea driven. We dug deeply into the operating contexts of many idea-driven organizations, to learn how they accomplished what they did. We also looked at organizations that were just taking their first steps toward becoming idea driven and followed them in near-real time to get a richer understanding of precisely what *works*, and what *does not,* along the way. At the same time, our work with leaders and managers who asked for help allowed us to test, refine, and then retest the concepts and advice in this book.

In some ways this book is about instigating nothing short of a revolution in the way organizations are run. But at the same time, we have tried to lay out a logical, incremental, learn-as-you-go approach to creating an idea-driven organization. Still, this is not an easy journey, and managers choosing to take it will need courage and persistence, as the transformation will take time and effort. But the lessons in this book will guide them in making the necessary changes with far less pain than their pioneering predecessors, and to quickly producing significant bottom-line results.

The bottom line is this: Idea-driven organizations have many times the improvement and innovation capability of their traditional counterparts. If you learn how to tap the ideas of your front-line workers, you can truly break free of the reductionist "more with less" mindset. You and your employees will thrive in environments where you once would have struggled to survive.

A final note: A lot can be learned by failure. Because we want to share examples of failure without embarrassing the people involved, our policy was to disguise the names of people and institutions whose stories might be construed in any way as negative.

1

The Power in Front-Line Ideas

WHAT IS THE BIGGEST SHORTFALL in the way we practice management today? With all the money pouring into business schools and executive education, and all the books, articles and experts to consult, why do so many organizations still fall so painfully short of their potential? What have their leaders and managers been missing?

There is no single reason for the less-than-brilliant performance of these organizations, of course, but one limiting factor is clear. Very few managers know how to effectively tap the biggest source of performance improvement available to them—namely, the creativity and knowledge of the people who work for them.

Every day, these people see problems and opportunities that their managers do not. They are full of ideas to save money or time; increase revenue; make their jobs easier; improve productivity, quality, and the customer experience; or make their organizations better in some other way.

For more than a century, people have dabbled with various approaches to promoting employee ideas, but with little real success. In recent years, however, the picture has changed. As we shall see, companies with the best idea systems in the world now routinely implement twenty, fifty, or even a hundred ideas per person per year. As a result they perform at extraordinarily high levels and are able to consistently deliver innovative new

1

products and services. Their customers enjoy working with them, and they are rewarding places to work.

This book is about how to build such an organization—an *idea-driven organization*—one designed and led to systematically seek and implement large numbers of (mostly small) ideas from *everyone,* but particularly from the people on the front lines. We are aware, of course, that many organizations are famous for their innovativeness but are *not* idea driven in our sense, because the preponderance of their ideas comes from a handful of highly creative departments or perhaps a lone genius. But however successful these organizations already are, they would be even more successful, and more sustainably innovative, if they were to become idea driven.

As an example of an idea-driven organization, let us look at Brasilata, which has been consistently named as one of the most innovative companies in Brazil by the FINEP (Financiadora de Estudos e Projetos), that country's science and development agency. Surprisingly, Brasilata is in the steel can industry, a two-hundred-year-old industry that was viewed as mature before the Soviet Union launched *Sputnik* in 1957. And yet 75 percent of Brasilata's products either are protected by patents or have been developed within the last five years. How can a company in such a mature industry be as innovative as Brazil's more well-known and high-flying technology, aerospace, energy, cosmetics, and fashion companies? Every year, Brasilata's nearly 1,000 "inventors" (the job titles of its front-line employees) come up with some 150,000 ideas, 90 percent of which are implemented.

Building an idea-driven organization such as Brasilata is not easy. There is a lot to know, much of which is counterintuitive. It took almost twenty years for Antonio Texeira, Brasilata's CEO, to build the processes and culture capable of this kind of idea performance. He and his leadership team had no readily available models to follow, no classes they could attend, and no experts to call for advice. They had to figure things out as they went.

Today, there is a small but growing number of idea-driven organizations, and their collective experiences allow us to ferret out what *works* and what *doesn't* when it comes to managing front-line ideas. This book lays out the general principles involved and describes how to methodically transform an ordinary organization into one that is idea driven. But before we get into how to do this, let us get a better sense of the power of front-line ideas by delving in some detail into another idea-driven organization—a company in Sweden whose idea system has won several national awards.

THE CLARION-STOCKHOLM HOTEL

The Clarion-Stockholm is a four-star hotel located in the center of Stockholm. It routinely averages more than fifty ideas per year from each of its employees—about one idea per person per week. One reason that Clarion employees are able to come up with so many ideas is that they have been trained to look for problems and opportunities to improve. For example, every time a guest complains, asks a question, or seems confused, staff members do all they can to fully understand the issue. If staffers have an idea to address the issue, they enter it into a special computer application. If not, they enter just the raw problem. Each department has a weekly idea meeting to review its ideas and problems, and decide on the actions it wants to take on each of them.

We met with several bartenders and went through all of their department's ideas from a randomly selected month. A sample of them is listed in Table 1.1.

As you read through these ideas, notice five things. First, the ideas are responding to problems and opportunities that are easily seen by the bar staff, but not so readily by their managers. How would the managers know that customers are asking for organic cocktails (Tess's idea) or vitamin shots (Fredrik's idea), or that the bartenders could serve more beer if an extra beer tap were added (Marin's idea)? Such insights come much more easily to employees who are serving the customers directly.

Second, most of the ideas are small and straightforward. They don't require much work to analyze and are inexpensive to implement. How difficult is it for the conference sales department to give the bartenders a "heads-up" that it will be meeting in the bar with a customer who is considering booking a major event (Nadia's idea)? And how hard is it to increase the font size of the print on coupons given to conference participants so as to clarify what they mean (Marco's idea) or to give the restaurant staff a tasting of the new bar cocktails so they can sell them more effectively to their diners (Tim's idea)?

TABLE 1.1   Ideas from the Clarion-Stockholm bar

Marco	Get maintenance to drill three holes in the floor behind the bar and install pipes so bartenders can drop bottles directly into the recycling bins in the basement.
Reza	When things are slow in the bar, mix drinks at the tables so the guests get a show.
Nadia	Many customers ask if we serve afternoon tea. Currently, there is no hotel in the entire south of Stockholm that does. I suggest we start doing this.
Tess	Have an organic cocktail. Customers often ask for them, and we don't offer one.
Nadia	Clarion conference and event sales staff often meet prospective customers in the bar. Give the bar staff information in advance about the prospects so they can be on alert and do something special.
Tim	Whenever the bar introduces a new cocktail, have a tasting for the restaurant staff, just as the restaurant always does when a new menu or menu item is introduced, so servers know what they are selling.
Fredrik	When the bar opens at 9:30 in the morning, many guests ask for vitamin shots (special blends of fruit juices). Put these on the menu.
Nadia	Have maintenance build some shelves in an unused area in the staff access corridor behind the bar for glasses. Currently, there is so little space for glasses in the bar that they are stored upstairs in the kitchen, and it takes 30 minutes, several times a night, for one of the two bartenders to go and get glasses, which means lost sales.
Marco	In the upstairs bar, we have to spend an hour bringing up all the alcohol from downstairs when we open and putting it away when we close. We wouldn't have to do this if locks were installed on the cabinets in the bar.
Marin	On our receipts, when guests pay with Eurocard, it says "Euro." This confuses many guests, who think they have been charged in euros instead of kronor. Get the accounting department to contact our Eurocard provider to see if we can change the header on the receipts.
Nadia	The bartending staff often act as concierges, telling people about the hotel, local shops, restaurants, and attractions, and giving directions. We have a concierge video that we show on our website. Offer this on the TVs in all hotel rooms.
Tess	Currently we close at 10 p.m. on Sundays, and many guests complain about this. Because we have a red dot on our liquor license from a single violation many years ago, we must have four security guards in the bar to be open after 10 on Sundays, and this is too expensive. Apply to have red dot removed, and then we can stay open with only one security guard.

TABLE 1.1 *(continued)* Ideas from the Clarion-Stockholm bar

Nadia	The late night security guards are sometimes curt and rude to the customers (the security service is subcontracted). These guards should be required to take the same "Attitude at Clarion" training that all Clarion staff take.
Marco	Increase the font size and make clearer that the coupons that conferences give out are for *discounts* at the bar, not for *free drinks*.
Nadia	Have the kitchen mark the prewrapped ham sandwiches that the bar sells. Bar staff currently have to cut them in half to tell the difference between them and the ham-and-cheese sandwiches.
Marin	Put an extra beer tap in the bar, so we can sell more beer. Currently, there is only one, and it is a bottleneck.
Nadia	Have maintenance put some sandpaper safety strips on the handicapped ramp in the bar. Children currently use it as a slide, and the bar staff has to deal with minor scrapes and cuts on a daily basis.
Nadia	Give the bar staff information about how many guests are staying in the hotel, so they can stock and staff the bar appropriately.

Third, the ideas are neither scattershot nor self-serving. They systematically drive performance improvement in key strategic areas for the hotel. They *improve customer service, increase productivity,* and make the bar a *better place to work*—in many cases doing all three at the same time. Before Marco's idea to drill three holes for tubes through the floor to allow the bar staff to drop recyclable cans and bottles directly into bins in the basement, once an hour a bartender had to lug a plastic tub of empties down long hallways and a flight of stairs to the basement, and then separate them into three different bins. This chore took a bartender away from serving customers for roughly ten minutes. One bartender commented that whenever one of them left the bar during a busy period to empty the recyclables tub, "You could watch sales go down." As their ideas free up time from unpleasant and non-value-adding work, the bartenders can do more for the customers, such as giving them a show at their tables when they order special mixed drinks (Reza's idea). And imagine how much more the upstairs bartenders look forward to their work when they do not have to begin their day by lugging the entire bar stock upstairs, and finish it by returning the bar stock to the special locked storeroom downstairs (Marco's idea). Making the hotel a better place for staff to work also affects the way they interact with their customers.

Fourth, these ideas pick up on important but intangible aspects of the bar's operations and environment. How many customers will no longer be driven away by rude security guards or rowdy children sliding down the handicapped ramp (Nadia's ideas)? In the hospitality industry, these intangibles often determine whether customers return or not.

Fifth, taken as a whole, the ideas illustrate the profound understanding the staff has of the bar's capabilities and customers, an understanding that only people working on the front lines can possess.

While the list of ideas from the bar is certainly impressive, what is more impressive is that every department in the Clarion-Stockholm implements a similar list of ideas every month and has been doing so for a number of years. Each of these ideas enhances the hotel in some small way, and over time their cumulative impact is huge. This level of idea performance does not happen by accident. It takes a leadership team that (1) appreciates the power of front-line ideas to move their organization in a desired direction, (2) is willing to make them a priority, (3) aligns the hotel's systems and policies to support them, (4) holds managers accountable for encouraging and implementing them, and (5) provides the necessary resources to run an idea-driven organization. The payoff, in this case, is a hotel capable of delivering better service at a more competitive price, a fact that is certainly noticed and appreciated by its guests. On one of our visits to Stockholm, when Sweden was feeling the impact of the global recession, we couldn't get rooms at the Clarion. The hotel was fully booked for most of the next *nine months*.

Employee ideas have certainly helped the Clarion in a number of important ways. But what many leaders want to know is this: how big an impact can a good idea system really have? Just across Stockholm, we found a company that had actually measured this impact.

THE IMPACT OF FRONT-LINE IDEAS: THE 80/20 PRINCIPLE

Several years ago, Coca-Cola Stockholm was struggling with a messy problem on its half-liter Coke bottling line. After being filled and capped, the bottles would zoom around a ninety-degree corner before passing an electronic eye that would scan each bottle in order to assure that it had been properly filled. If not, an air piston would activate and push the improperly filled bottle off the line. As long as the bottles were properly spaced, the process worked quite well. Unfortunately, the bottles would sometimes bunch together as they rounded the corner. Then, when the air piston pushed a bottle into the rejection chute, the next bottle (which was in contact with the first) would be shifted slightly, sometimes causing it to hit the edge of the chute, tip over, and block the line. Ten bottles per second would then slam into the fallen bottle and Coke would fly everywhere, creating a huge mess and ruining many bottles before the operator could stop the line. This disruption to production occurred two or three times per day.

Two Six Sigma black belt project teams had failed to solve the problem, which they determined to be caused by friction between the bottles and the corner guide.[1] The teams had fiddled with many variables—the line speed, different kinds of lubricating strips along the curve guide, and the spacing of the bottles—but with little success. In the end, both teams could only come up with faster ways to clean up the mess after each incident.

Ironically, after the black belt teams failed, the problem was solved by a simple idea from one of the bottling-line workers. His solution was to reduce the contact surface area between the guide and the bottles. By slipping a steel washer in between the guide and its mounting bracket, the guide was cocked slightly inward so that only its upper edge touched the bottle (see Figure 1.1). This lowered the friction enough to keep the bottles from bunching. The idea saved a lot of hassle cleaning up the spills, reduced downtime on the bottling line, and eliminated the need to dispose of about $15,000 worth of damaged products per year. And this was only one of 1,720 front-line ideas implemented that year.

FIGURE 1.1 Half-liter bottle idea

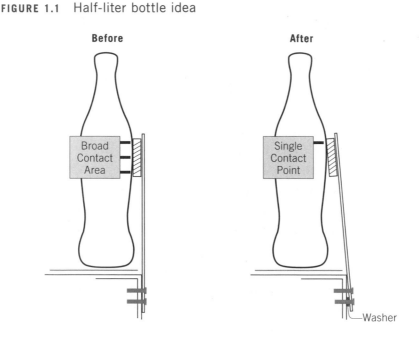

Interestingly, a few years before, Coca-Cola headquarters had required all corporate-owned bottlers to implement Six Sigma as a way to drive improvement. Each unit was expected to (1) train a cadre of black and green belts, (2) focus on Six Sigma improvement projects that would generate large documentable monetary savings, and (3) strive for high bottling capacity utilization. The implementation of Six Sigma on top of an effective idea system provided a rare opportunity to compare the relative impact of *management-driven* and *front-line-driven* approaches to improvement. Before joining Coca-Cola, the managing director had worked at Scania, the Swedish truck maker, which placed strong emphasis on front-line ideas. When she arrived at Coca-Cola Stockholm, one of her first actions had been to put a high-performing idea system in place. By the time the Six Sigma initiative was fully operational, the bottling unit was implementing fifteen ideas per person per year.

The managing director used the exhibit shown in Figure 1.2 to illustrate the relative contribution of each source of cost-saving improvements.

In 2007, for example, two black belt and five green belt Six Sigma projects were completed, for savings that totaled 2.5 million Swedish kronor (SEK) (1 USD was then about 6 SEK). But the 1,720 front-line ideas generated some 8 million SEK in savings, or 76 percent of overall improvement. Armed with this insight, the company increased its emphasis on employee ideas; and in 2008, this percentage increased to 83 percent. In 2010, the company stopped tracking the cost savings from front-line ideas because the financial benefits from them were clear.

All these ideas helped Coca-Cola Stockholm surpass its peers in almost all the primary performance categories for bottling plants. Globally, it ranked first in productivity, quality, safety, environmental performance, and customer fulfillment rate. The only key metric in which Stockholm was not the top performer was *capacity utilization*. Standing in the mid–60 percent utilization range, its rank on this metric was merely average. The managing director told us that this was because the large number of front-line improvement ideas was constantly increasing her bottling capacity.

The Coca-Cola improvement data reflect what we have come to call the *80/20 Principle of Improvement*: roughly 80 percent of an organization's

FIGURE 1.2 Coca-Cola Stockholm improvement results

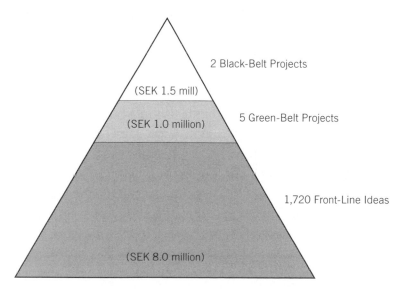

2 Black-Belt Projects

(SEK 1.5 mill)

(SEK 1.0 million)

5 Green-Belt Projects

1,720 Front-Line Ideas

(SEK 8.0 million)

performance improvement potential lies in front-line ideas, and only 20 percent in management-driven initiatives.

Managers can find it very difficult to accept the fact that front-line ideas offer *four times* the improvement potential of their own. But we have witnessed many examples. A case in point: Several years ago, a U.S. Navy technical support base was being pushed hard to increase its levels of support, while at the same time pressure on the defense budget was forcing it to make severe cuts. The base commander saw a high-performing idea system as a way to deal with these conflicting demands and asked us for help.

During one of our early training sessions, several upper and middle managers expressed skepticism about devoting valuable leadership attention to getting front-line ideas. In the ensuing discussion, we brought up the 80/20 principle and pointed out that if the laboratory did not go after front-line ideas, it would be trying to make headway with at most 20 percent of its innovation and cost-saving capability. One of the skeptics, the base's top improvement expert and a Lean Six Sigma Master Black Belt, suddenly got up and left the room.

He returned a short time later and reported that he had thought the 80/20 assertion was overstated, so he had left to check it against the base's own data. While the base's Lean Six Sigma program was intended primarily as a tool for management-driven improvement, it did allow "grassroots" projects to be initiated by front-line staff. The Master Black Belt had pulled the data on the previous year's projects and separated out the savings from the grassroots projects. The leadership team had budgeted $6.8 million in savings from Lean Six Sigma—$5.4 million (79.4 percent) from management-initiated projects and $1.4 million (20.6 percent) from front-line initiated projects. But the actual savings turned out to be only $1.2 million (17.6 percent) from management-initiated projects, and $5.6 million (82.4 percent) from grassroots projects—the opposite of what had been anticipated.

Ironically, when we first encountered the 80/20 phenomenon many years ago at a Dana auto parts manufacturing plant in Cape Girardeau, Missouri, we didn't believe it, either. At the time, the three-hundred-person operation was implementing some thirty-six ideas per person per year. While we were talking with the plant manager, he casually mentioned that 80 percent of his operation's improvement came from front-line ideas. We had already studied and worked with idea systems for over a decade by then and, even with everything we had seen, didn't take his statement literally. To us, it was simply a self-effacing comment and a generous recognition of his front-line people. But it did get us thinking about the relative impact of front-line ideas. We started collecting data whenever we came across it, and over the years have found it to be surprisingly consistent. Across organizations in services, manufacturing, health care, and government, 80 percent of an organization's improvement potential lies in front-line ideas.

In our experience, when leaders become convinced of the validity of the 80/20 principle, they realize what they have been missing and want a high-performing idea system in their organizations. However, they need to be careful. There is a lot more involved in getting these ideas than simply setting up an idea process and layering it onto an existing organization.

CREATING AN IDEA-DRIVEN ORGANIZATION

Over the last several decades, U.S. furniture makers have been hit hard by global competition. Low-cost foreign competitors have forced many furniture makers out of business or obliged them to source their production overseas. Today, more than 75 percent of all wood and metal furniture sold in the United States is imported. In North Carolina alone, more than two hundred furniture manufacturers have gone out of business, and fifty thousand furniture workers have lost their jobs. Yet one company in that state, Hickory Chair, did very well throughout these hard times.

After the sudden death of the company's forty-nine-year-old president in 1996, Jay Reardon, the vice president of marketing, was asked to take over as president. His first step was to conduct a thorough analysis of the company's situation, from which he documented a trend that had been troubling him for some time. Over the previous decade, annual unit sales (a "unit" is one piece of furniture) had dropped from 137,000 to 87,000. The main reason Hickory Chair was still in business was that it had been able to increase its prices every year to compensate for these declining unit sales. This had pushed the average unit price for its furniture from around $300 to over $900. But Hickory's ability to continue raising prices was coming to an end. Several lower-cost competitors had recently moved into Hickory's niche of eighteenth- and nineteenth-century reproductions and were already undercutting its prices by 20 to 25 percent.

Reardon realized that in order to survive, Hickory had to figure out how to deliver much more value to its customers. It had to significantly lower costs, improve quality, and increase its responsiveness. Reardon openly admitted that he had limited knowledge about how furniture was made, but he did know how to approach the overall challenge. He had previously worked at Milliken Corporation, a textile company that, during his time there, was implementing more than eighty ideas per employee per year.[2] After four generations of the Milliken family's running the company in a heavily top-down manner, CEO Roger Milliken had transformed it into one driven by employee ideas, radically improving its performance in the process.

When Reardon proposed a similar transformative initiative to involve Hickory's front-line workers in improving the company, he encountered stiff resistance from his leadership team. Furniture-making companies in the United States had a long-standing tradition of authoritarian management, and Hickory Chair was no exception. Adding further to the challenge, several of his vice presidents who had been passed over for the company's top job when Reardon was chosen were actively undermining his initiatives.

After struggling with his management team for almost a year, Reardon decided to take his plans directly to the front lines. He assembled the entire workforce of some four hundred employees at a local community college and showed them how the company's unit sales were dropping while its prices were going up. He explained that these trends were unsustainable and told them that he needed their help. Then he introduced his concept of an idea program.

Reardon began taking regular walks through the plant and talking with his workers. Whenever an employee approached him with a problem, Reardon made certain it was fixed. When someone pointed out to him that the supervisors were using the bathrooms in the front offices because the factory bathrooms were in such bad shape, he checked them out and immediately ordered maintenance to fix them up and keep them clean. When informed about blatant misconduct by some supervisors—who among other things were clocking in girlfriends who were not at work and giving overtime preferentially to friends—Reardon investigated the allegations and ended up firing several of them.

He also went to work on his management team. He gave several of his more recalcitrant vice presidents an option: they could be fired immediately, or they could stay on for up to six months while looking for new jobs, on condition that they not do anything to harm the company or hinder Reardon's initiatives. Over the next couple of years, about 70 percent of his managers either were asked to leave or chose to leave because their management styles no longer meshed with an environment of highly empowered front-line workers. In the process, an entire layer of management was eliminated.

About two years after Reardon had launched his idea initiative, the rate of improvement began to slow. After reading in several books about the work of the Toyota Supplier Support Center (TSSC)—the organization Toyota set up to develop its North American suppliers—Reardon contacted it to see if it would be willing to help Hickory. Even though Hickory was not a Toyota supplier, the legendary Toyota *sensei* Hajime Ohba agreed to come to North Carolina for a day and see what he could do.

When Ohba arrived, Reardon and several managers led him on a tour of the plant. At one point, while they were talking, an alarm went off. The managers ignored it and continued to talk. Ohba interrupted them: "What's that?"

"The line-stop alarm."

Ohba walked over to the line and asked one of the employees, "Why did the line stop?"

"The drive chain was clogged with lint."

"Why did the chain get clogged with lint?" Ohba inquired.

"We didn't clean the lint trap out because our supervisor told us we didn't have time. We needed to get production out."

Ohba smiled, "Well, you have plenty of time now."

He then turned to the managers and said, "The reason the line went down was that the supervisor prevented the operators from doing what they knew was right."

Reardon recalled this incident as a defining moment for his managers and him. "We were like a covey of quail, standing there yapping. The alarm went off and we continued to talk. Mr. Ohba, however, went directly to the source of the problem and began pushing for a solution. The employees already knew what needed to happen. We realized that our supervisors were often just getting in the way."

Over the next decade, Hickory Chair's quality, responsiveness, and innovativeness improved dramatically. Hickory didn't just survive—it thrived. Work-in-process inventory was cut more than 90 percent, and lead times went from sixteen weeks to a week and a half, allowing the company to almost entirely eliminate finished goods inventory. Several new designer furniture lines were introduced, and customization options were added to 90 percent of the company's furniture with no increase in delivery lead time. Half of the manufacturing that Hickory had been outsourcing to Asia was brought back in house. Except for the 2008 recession, annual sales grew at double-digit rates, and profit margins increased while prices were held steady. Hickory's return on assets (ROA) increased to almost *50 percent.*

Notice that Reardon did not just set up a process for getting front-line ideas and wait for the ideas to pour in. He had a lot of things to fix, both with his people and in his organization. He needed to correct a number of serious problems that would get in the way of improvement, to recast his management team, to learn and apply the best practices in idea management, to gain the trust and respect of his front-line workers, and to train and then empower them.

WHY ARE IDEA-DRIVEN ORGANIZATIONS SO RARE?

An obvious question arises. Given that organizations like Hickory Chair have achieved extraordinary results by tapping the ideas of their front-line people, why aren't leaders around the world falling all over themselves to do the same thing?

The answer has two parts. First, as we saw with Hickory Chair, building an idea-driven organization takes a lot of hard work. Second, trusting front-line employees to do what is best for the organization runs counter to traditional management practice.

An interesting case in point was the time we were asked to help a New England utility that was under tremendous pressure to cut costs. We began by spending several days looking at various parts of the company to learn how it worked. At one point, we found ourselves talking to a group of workers and supervisors in a regional depot where the company stored wire, poles, and equipment for repair and maintenance work. They laughed as they told us about the constant stream of ludicrous cost-cutting measures that had been coming down from above. One they found particularly comical was a recent policy aimed at reducing the inventory of transformers held in each depot. The policy mandated that each depot keep on hand no more than two transformers of each size. But even a light rainfall, the workers told us, could wipe out the stocks of the most commonly used smaller transformers, forcing the workers to install bigger more expensive ones in their place. In fact, just the previous week, they had been forced to deploy extra crews and equipment to jury-rig a brand new $500,000 transformer to replace a $2,000 one. And after the smaller transformers were ordered and received, the crews had to be sent back out, this time to take out the larger transformers and install the smaller ones.

The utility company managers undoubtedly thought their new policy was sound. And with the pressures they were under, it is easy to see how excess inventory would be a tempting target to free up much-needed operating cash and to cut costs. It is also easy to imagine how these managers reviewed the inventory of supplies at the depots and focused in on transformers, because transformers are expensive. So far, so good. Their mistake was to put their new inventory policy in place without consulting the people who understood how it would impact operations.

The new transformer policy was made at a distance, based on data that told only part of the story. But at the same time as these managers were patting themselves on the back for their cost-cutting brilliance, all they had really accomplished was to drive up the company's operating expenses and create a great deal of stress and non-value-adding work for its line crews.

The utility managers' actions contrast sharply with Jay Reardon's approach to the same type of problem at Hickory Chair. He, too, looked at the data and realized that he needed to cut costs. But then he went directly to his front-line people who had the specific knowledge needed to actually do so. While the New England utility managers identified the problem, came up with a solution, and ordered its implementation, Reardon identified the problem, shared it with his front-line people, and asked them for their ideas on how best to solve it. Instead of a command-and-control approach that was *top directed* and *top driven,* his approach was *top directed* but *bottom driven.* Reardon got the desired results. Those utility company executives did not.

The Nobel Prize–winning economist Friedrich Hayek provided insight into why the top-directed but bottom-driven approach is so much more effective.[3] He separated knowledge into two types: *aggregate knowledge* about the organization, and *knowledge of the particular circumstances of time and place.* Aggregate knowledge is what top managers tend to have. It comes from dealing with high-level data and performance numbers. These numbers are derived by quantifying, simplifying, and then combining the results of all the activities that are taking place across the entire organization and outside it. Such data provide a good picture of overall performance and trends, and are needed for making strategic-level decisions and setting the organization's direction. This was how Reardon used the data. But, as he knew, top managers generally do not have much of the other type of knowledge, because they do not see most of the details from which their aggregate information is produced. As a result, they are poorly equipped to make the many smaller decisions that actually *drive* the outcomes they are after. When they do make these decisions, their resulting commands give them only the *illusion* of control.

Managers can easily fall into the trap of believing that they know best and that their jobs are to issue orders and make certain those orders are followed. In Chapter 2, we discuss the powerful forces that cause so many people to gravitate to this command-and-control thinking as they rise up in their organizations. We then address what is needed to counteract these forces and how to develop a management team that is capable of building and leading an idea-driven organization.

REALIGNING THE ORGANIZATION FOR IDEAS

We often give participants in our seminars the following assignment: identify a bottom-up improvement or innovation in your organization, interview the people who championed it, and briefly document their stories. When the participants present their findings to the group, invariably a litany of horror stories emerges as they tell of the heroic lengths their subjects had to go to in order to overcome managerial indifference or opposition, burdensome policies and rules, uncooperative people in other departments, key players not wanting to change, and a host of other ridiculous and petty behavioral and institutional barriers. At some point in the process of listening to these stories, someone always asks, "Why are these organizations and their managers making it so difficult for their people to implement good ideas?" Bingo!

Hero stories are a recurring theme in innovation and improvement. After years of operating in a top-down manner that emphasizes control and conformance, organizations are rife with obstacles to bottom-up ideas that their champions are forced to overcome. Perhaps the most challenging part of building an idea-driven organization is *realigning* it for ideas—in other words, rooting out and eliminating misalignments that are impeding the flow of ideas—so the organization can move beyond the "champions battling barriers" model of innovation and improvement.

In many cases, these misalignments are problems that have subtly plagued performance for years, but they have been tolerated because their impact has been difficult to pin down. But once an idea system is in place and the volume of ideas ramps up, the impact of these misalignments becomes much clearer, and managers can no longer ignore them.

The process of realigning an organization for ideas is never ending. Initially, many misalignments will be easy to spot as even the simplest ideas experience petty implementation delays. Examples of this from organizations we have worked with include a specialty manufacturer where it was not possible for workers and supervisors to get a few dollars to test or implement small ideas, a national luxury goods retail chain where even minor improvements needed to be approved by committees or signed off on by countless managers, a European insurance company with a three-month backlog for even the smallest IT change request, and a federal agency whose IT backlog was three years!

Less obvious barriers will often emerge only as the organization becomes more sophisticated at managing ideas. For example, some of the least visible and hardest-to-correct misalignments arise from poorly conceptualized or outdated *policies*. Policies are an important part of running any organization, but as we shall discuss, they often have unintended consequences. They are made by people throughout the organization who are trying to deal with various situations from their own perspectives—people who don't typically consider their policies' impact on the flow of ideas.

Chapters 3 and 4 discuss common misalignments and how to correct them. Chapter 3 explains the mechanisms that idea-driven organizations use to focus their front-line ideas on key strategic goals. Chapter 4 is about how to realign an organization's management systems to enable the smooth flow of ideas. An important section of this chapter is about the development of policies, where we provide a brief primer on how to make more effective policies and how to deal with bad ones. In particular, we describe in some detail the "Kill Stupid Rules" process developed by a U.S. regional bank to modify or eliminate dysfunctional policies.

EFFECTIVE IDEA PROCESSES

A few years ago, a senior vice president at a national specialty retailer decided to conduct a campaign for employee ideas in his unit. He commissioned an expensive inspirational video, staged a big high-energy launch event, and pressured his managers to go after employee ideas. Over the next two months, his people submitted more than eight hundred ideas. The campaign appeared to have been a rousing success. But five months later, after the CEO had independently invited us in to implement a companywide idea system, only *six* of the eight hundred ideas had been implemented. Despite this, and the fact that several of his colleagues told us that they regarded his initiative as a spectacular failure, the senior vice president remained upbeat. He didn't understand the damage he had done. He had staked his credibility on a poorly thought-out effort that had ended up using less than 1 percent of the ideas that his people had given him. More than 90 percent of the suggesters never even received a response. It is hard to imagine how he could have more effectively undermined his people's trust in his willingness to listen to their ideas.

That senior vice president had not realized that there was a lot more involved in managing ideas than simply collecting them. Employees were not told what kinds of ideas were important, he did not allocate any time or resources to evaluate and implement the ideas that came in, and his managers were thrown into the campaign without any proper direction or training, which left them unsure of their roles and without some of the skills they would need.

The mistakes this executive made are not unusual. Over the years, we have watched many leaders set up idea processes believing that they will be easy to get up and running. They are unaware of the existence of high-performance idea processes, let alone what is needed to develop and launch one. From the outset, their initiatives are condemned to delivering mediocre results or to failing outright.

Chapter 5 explains how high-performing idea processes work. Although all such systems share the same principles, in practice they can look quite different. Every organization is unique: each has its own culture, cast of characters, operating systems and norms, capabilities, and history. A good idea system is not a stand-alone program. It has to be designed to work in concert with a lot of other parts of the organization. Chapter 6 is a step-by-step walk through the process of designing and launching a high-performance idea system. We discuss the pitfalls and issues that often arise, and provide tactics for dealing with them.

GETTING MORE AND BETTER IDEAS

One of the authors recently had an interesting experience at a local diner. As the waitress took his drink order, she put down a paper placemat, a knife, and a fork that had a large piece of fried egg encrusted between its prongs. She glanced at the fork, then at the author, and walked away.

Had the author been eating breakfast at the Ritz-Carlton, the dirty fork would not have made it anywhere near the table. The hotel trains its employees to be sensitive to even the slightest service problem. What was not a problem for the waitress in the diner would have been a major issue at the Ritz-Carlton.

Ideas begin with problems. If people don't see problems, they won't be thinking about how to solve them. Thus *problem sensitivity* is a key driver of ideas.

When an organization starts up a high-performing idea system, there is often an early surge of ideas directed at problems that have been bothering people for a long time. But after all the obvious problems have been addressed, employees start to run out of ideas. The remedy is training— training designed to create sensitivity to new types of problems.

In Chapter 7, we describe a variety of proven methods that idea-driven organizations have used to help their people see new and different kinds of problems, so that they can come up with greater numbers of more useful ideas. *Idea activators,* for example, introduce people to new ways to improve their work. *Idea mining* is used to extract fresh perspectives from ideas that have already been proposed. These and other methods we discuss, which can be delivered in surprisingly brief training modules, allow both employees and managers to approach idea generation with a sense of *abundance* of improvement opportunities rather than a sense of *scarcity*.

IDEA SYSTEMS AND INNOVATIVENESS

A few years ago, one of our former students was promoted to vice president at a Wall Street investment bank, and was tasked with making the bank more innovative. He called us and asked, "What should I do? Where should I start?"

Many leaders struggle with those questions and end up doing a variety of generally ineffective things in the name of innovation. For the majority, their first step should be to set up a high-performance idea system. It may seem strange that a leader looking for more breakthrough innovations should make it a top priority to go after ideas from the front lines. But for a number of reasons, the ability to produce successful breakthrough products and services on a consistent basis depends on the ability to tap large numbers of smaller front-line ideas.

Several years ago, we had the opportunity to track the development of one of Brasilata's award-winning steel cans (Brasilata is the Brazilian company discussed in the beginning of this chapter that was averaging some 150 ideas per employee). The idea for it originated with an accounting clerk when a product designer happened to show her the prototype of a new can. She commented to him that with some minor modifications it would make a handy container for several common cooking ingredients she used. Her observation was opportune, for at the time Brasilata was producing cans primarily for nonfood products, and its management was looking for products that could be used to expand its offerings in the food market.

As we were tracking how the new can had been developed, at one point we found ourselves talking with a group of production workers who were fabricating it. One of the can's features required some particularly clever processing, which we were trying to understand.

"By the way," we asked, "who thought of this feature?"

The question triggered a short and intense discussion in Portuguese. Then one of the workers turned to us and said, "We can't remember who came up with that idea, us or R&D."

We went back to the R&D department to find out. No one there could remember, either!

As this story illustrates, ideas flow freely across Brasilata. Innovation pervades every aspect of what it does. It has been able to develop sophisticated technologies that are much more flexible than commercially available alternatives—and at a fraction of their cost. All this has allowed Brasilata to generate a continuous stream of breakthrough products that its competitors cannot duplicate.

In Chapter 8, we explain the multifaceted interplay between innovation and front-line ideas, an interplay that most managers are not aware of. As a result, their organizations are far less innovative than they could be. It is ironic that the most powerful enabler of innovativeness for most organizations is the last thing their leaders would think of.

2

A Different Kind
of Leadership

MORE THAN A quarter century ago, Professor Fred Luthans of the University of Nebraska published an intriguing study that found a significant difference between how "successful" managers (those who got promoted rapidly) and "effective" managers (those whose units performed well) spent their time.[1] The managers who were promoted rapidly spent much more time networking and politicking, while their more effective colleagues spent their time building their units and developing their people. In short, Luthans found that organizations were promoting the wrong types of managers. And because the managers who got promoted the fastest were also the ones who ended up in top leadership positions, Luthans's study was an implicit indictment of how most organizations chose their leaders.

Although his study was conducted a while ago, we believe his findings are just as valid today. These findings alone might explain why leaders who pay attention to their front-line people are so rare, but the picture is actually much worse. Even when organizations do promote the right managers, as these managers rise up the hierarchy, a host of situational forces come to bear on them that can easily undermine their respect for the people on the front lines, and hence cause them to disregard the value in their ideas.

In this chapter, we discuss the dysfunctional behaviors that people often exhibit as they gain power and the reasons that such behaviors arise. We then turn to how idea-driven organizations counteract this problem and keep their managers engaged with their front-line people and valuing their ideas.

WHY LEADERS ARE OFTEN BLIND TO FRONT-LINE IDEAS

Consider the constant reminders of their superiority that managers are bombarded with in the course of their daily work. They wear the suits, they have the private offices, they are the ones chosen for promotion, they are more highly educated and paid significantly more than their subordinates, and everyone defers to them. They are the ones in charge. With all of these signals continually reminding them that they are superior to their employees, it is easy for managers to come to believe that they actually are. And such a belief can lead them into some highly dysfunctional behaviors.

One way that managers' feelings of superiority manifest themselves is in excessive pay disparities and inappropriate perks. More than a century ago, J. P. Morgan observed an interesting pattern in his client companies. Those having excessive pay differences between levels in their hierarchies did not perform as well. Consequently, he would not invest in a company if pay differences from level to level were more than 30 percent. Morgan had put his finger on something important. If differences between levels in a company become too great, its intangible fabric of trust, communication, and respect unravels, which introduces enormous hidden costs.[2] From the point of view of ideas, the ability of managers to listen to those who work for them is greatly reduced, as is the willingness of their subordinates to offer ideas.

We encountered a good example of the detrimental impact of extreme differences between levels on the flow of ideas while helping a European port and logistics company with its idea system. We arrived at the port in a blinding wet snowstorm to find the parking lot full. But directly in front of the headquarters building there was a row of mostly open spaces. Furthermore, these spaces were covered by a blue awning, which extended conveniently all the way to the front entrance. We couldn't believe our luck—the visitors' parking was right up front and protected from the weather! We pulled into one of the open spots and began getting out of the car. A well-dressed receptionist bustled out from the lobby and confronted us: "I'm afraid you can't park there. It's for top managers only." We got back in the car, circulated some more, and eventually squeezed into a spot at the back of the lot. We got soaked as we ran into the building.

The right to park under the blue awning turned out to be a jealously guarded top management perk. The company's headquarters were on the Adriatic coast, near the Italian Alps. In winter, it snowed and rained a lot, and in summer the hot Mediterranean sun baked any car left out in the open. That awning spoke volumes. On a daily basis, it reinforced top managers' perceptions that they were somehow more worthy than their employees—they should not have to get wet in the winter or climb into swelteringly hot cars in the summer—and it reminded employees of their second-class status.

We had been invited because the company was losing business to more nimble competitors, and top management had set up an idea system hoping to capture employee ideas to cut costs. Unfortunately, very few ideas were coming in and almost none were being implemented. The managing director and his team thought the problem lay somewhere in the mechanics of the idea system, but the real problem turned out to be the gap the management team had created between itself and the workers. The blue awning had been our first indication of this. No matter how much the leaders of this company tweaked their idea process, unless they changed their behavior, they were not going to get much help from their employees in making the company more competitive.

When the perks that arise from management feelings of superiority are out of public view, some of them can be ridiculous. In Riverside, California, one such perk revealed much about the attitude of the county executives toward their workers. County policy specified that all bathroom tissue purchased for county government bathrooms must be two-ply. Yet the county supervisor had quietly upgraded the toilet paper used in the bathrooms of the county's top executives to a more expensive and softer four-ply. A whistleblower "outed" this perk to the press just after the county announced that employees had to take a 10 percent pay cut in response to a budget crisis. After a storm of negative coverage of what the media dubbed "Bathroom Tissue Gate," the embarrassed officials sheepishly reverted back to two-ply.[3]

From reserved parking places to separate bathrooms, the last things managers need are extravagant status symbols that tell them that they are better than the people who work for them. Once they believe that, they can easily believe that they *know* better, too.

How Power Can Undermine Idea Leadership

Excessive perks and salary differentials are relatively easy to eliminate if an organization's leaders have the will to do so. Unfortunately, power has more destructive effects on people than causing them to overpay themselves or pamper themselves with soft bathroom tissue, and many of these effects are much less apparent.

A considerable amount of research has been done on how power affects people. A classic, and very revealing, study was done in the early 1970s by Stanford psychology professor Philip Zimbardo. He conducted what became an infamous experiment, now known as the Stanford Prison Experiment.[4] Together with his research team, Zimbardo built a mock prison in the basement of the psychology building. He recruited a pool of intelligent, healthy, and normal male students and randomly divided them into two groups: guards and prisoners. Great care was taken to re-create the power relationship between the guards and prisoners that is found in real prisons. On the day the experiment began, the prisoners-to-be were arrested as they went about their daily business by Palo Alto police officers. The prisoners were put in barred cells and placed "under the complete subjugation" of the guards. The experiment was continuously observed and both audio- and videotaped. Although it was scheduled to last two weeks, it quickly spun out of control and was aborted after only six days. The guards had become so abusive that the prisoners were in danger of mental and physical breakdown. Some of the video footage is shocking, and several of the "prisoners" suffered significant psychological problems for years afterward. Zimbardo would comment almost forty years later on the eerie similarities between the abuses during his prison experiment and the abuses in 2003 and 2004 at the Abu Ghraib prison in Iraq while U.S. forces were running the facility.[5] Ultimately, the experiment resulted in significant new understanding of how a situation's context can override people's natural dispositions and radically alter their behavior. It also led to major changes around the world in the rules governing human subject experimentation.

The provocative nature of Zimbardo's findings spurred considerable academic research on the effects of power on a person's behavior. One particularly enlightening follow-up study, for example, was done by Adam Galinsky, Deborah Gruenfeld, and Joe Magee (Gruenfeld was a colleague of Zimbardo's at Stanford).[6] As they noted:

The experience of holding power in a particular situation generates a constellation of characteristics and propensities that manifest themselves in affect, cognition, and behavior.

It is easy to see how some of these "characteristics and propensities" have a direct negative effect on a person's receptiveness to ideas from subordinates. For example:

- Power reduces the complexity of a person's thinking and his ability to consider alternatives.
- Power leads to objectification—that is, to seeing others as a means to an end as opposed to seeing them as real people.
- People with power listen less carefully and have difficulty taking into account what others already know.
- People with power do not regulate their behavior as much. They become egocentric and preoccupied with their own self-interest, which eclipses their awareness of the interests of others.
- People with power are less accurate in their estimates of the interests and positions of others, and less open to the perspectives of others.

In our own work, we often see power bringing out these tendencies and watch them undermine the trust and respect needed for an organization to operate effectively. Recently, we were hired by the new CEO of a large pharmaceutical company to design and lead an upper management development program aimed at improving the company's ability to innovate and improve. We began by spending a day interviewing managers and workers to build an understanding of the issues the program would need to address. A picture of a dysfunctional and demoralized organization quickly emerged, one ruled by fear. At the end of the day, we spent an hour and a half with the CEO in order to better understand his goals for the upcoming program. The CEO was very clear—he was not impressed with his managers and wanted them shaken up.

"I have set the goal of 30 percent sales growth for each of the next three years," he said, "and I need them to be able to keep up."

"How did you come up with that goal?"

"Actually, I just pulled it out of a hat," the CEO replied, with a smirk. Further probing revealed that he had given little thought to this stretch goal or whether it was even achievable. Was there enough market demand? What changes in the company's physical plant would be needed to produce the increased volume? Would the resources be available to expand capacity and to fund the increased sales volume? What increases in staff would be needed, and where? He had not considered any of these basic questions.

That night, the CEO invited us and the managers who would be participating in the program out to dinner. At one point, the conversation turned to a recent environmental incident at one of the company's plants. A large amount of hot liquid petroleum jelly had been accidentally released into the municipal wastewater treatment system, which had become clogged as the liquid cooled and gelled. As a result, two of the senior managers at the table had been summoned to a hearing the following morning and were worried that the company would lose its permit to use the municipal system. The CEO was completely unconcerned—in fact, he joked about the spill and made several derogatory remarks about the local environmental regulations. And then he boasted, "The first thing I did when I moved here [to an East Coast state with strict environmental rules] was to slip my garbage guy a couple of hundred bucks. Now I don't have to worry about recycling or hazardous waste—he'll take anything I put out." His leadership team was visibly stunned.

Over the course of the management training program, it became clear that the leadership team members did not trust or respect the CEO. They felt that he was out for himself and unwilling to address the company's real problems. But because several successful new products had been brought on line just as he joined the company, sales were strong and forecasts were rosy. As long as the CEO made sure the board heard only what he wanted them to, his job would be secure. He was a classic example of a "successful" manager in the Luthans sense, and he personified all the negative behaviors and cognitive limitations that power can bring out in a person.

FIGHTING BACK

In 2013, after a series of embarrassing public scandals involving top commanders, U.S. Army General Martin Dempsey, chairman of the Joint Chiefs of Staff, instituted a new "360-degree" evaluation system for senior officers—that is, an evaluation system in which input about their characters and competence would be sought from their direct subordinates and peers. According to the *New York Times:*[7]

> *General Dempsey said that evaluations of top officers needed to go beyond the traditional assessment of professional performance by superior officers alone . . . to assess both competence and character in a richer way. . . . The central role in national life played by the military since the attacks of Sept. 11, 2001—a time in which some general officers attained the stature, and entourages, of rock stars—put them in the spotlight. "Frankly, we've developed some bad habits," General Dempsey said. . . . "It's those bad habits we are seeking to overcome."*

The new evaluation regime was part of a broader overhaul of the way senior military leaders were to be selected and developed. Dempsey was attempting to stop his senior leaders from succumbing to the bad habits that come with power.

Fighting the forces that drive these bad habits takes place on two fronts. The first involves hiring and promoting the right managers, and the second involves keeping existing managers grounded so they continue to value their subordinates and treat them with respect.

Hiring and Promoting the Right People

Jay Reardon, president of Hickory Chair, the company whose dramatic turnaround was described in the last chapter, was very clear about what he looked for when hiring or promoting managers:

> *First, I look for people who are humble. Humility is not a weakness—it is a strength. I am careful to do the background work to make certain a candidate will be truly humble. How does he talk about his coworkers? How do they talk about him? Is he in the background supporting others and celebrating their accomplishments, or is he standing out front demanding all the attention?*

During interviews, Reardon listens carefully to how candidates discuss their work and other people. "If they talk primarily about business and the numbers, and all the great things they have accomplished, I eliminate them from serious consideration. But if they focus more on their people's contributions and accomplishments, then I look at them more seriously. I look for more 'we's and 'us's, and fewer 'I's and 'me's, in the way they talk."

We asked Jesus Echevarria, chief communications officer at Inditex, what characteristics his company looked for in its managers. "First of all, humility," he said. "A manager has to have the humility to listen to and respect other people's ideas if he expects to rise up in Inditex." (Afterward, we realized that Echevarria never did offer a second characteristic.) Inditex, best known for its Zara brand of "fast-fashion" stores, is headquartered in A Coruna, Spain, and is the world's largest clothing company with more than six thousand stores in seventy countries. Zara's business model is built around closely listening to customers and rapidly acting on the resulting information. It relies on its sales associates to observe what fashion-conscious customers are wearing and to listen to what they are requesting. Twice a week, headquarters calls each store to get its associates' observations and ideas. (We will discuss Zara's idea processes more fully in Chapter 3.) Echevarria emphasized that humble managers are necessary for a business model that is based on careful listening.

Amancio Ortega, founder and majority stockholder of Inditex, realized the importance of humility in managers at a very early age. He grew up poor and was forced to drop out of school at age twelve to work as a delivery boy for a women's clothing store. He was bothered by the fact that the store wasn't offering the types of clothing that its customers were asking for. He brought many improvement ideas to the store manager, but the manager never listened to him. Out of frustration, and while still in his teens, Ortega set up his own small clothing manufacturing company. By building a company that could listen extremely carefully to its customers and then respond very rapidly, Ortega would go on to become one of the richest men in the world.

To maintain its culture of humility, almost all of Inditex's hiring is done for entry-level positions, and most managers are promoted from within the company. The exceptions occur when specific professional skills are needed that are not available internally, and in these cases the company is very careful to fit the new recruits into its culture.

In the late 1990s, for example, when Inditex was preparing for both rapid global expansion and an initial public offering, it was forced to hire a number of high-powered managers from the outside. One of them was Jesus Vega de la Falla, the new director of HR. He had an MBA from IESE (ranked among the top business schools in the world) and had extensive management experience at both Hewlett-Packard and Banco Santander (a large global bank headquartered in Madrid). When he arrived on his first day at Inditex, he was met by the company's CEO, who informed him that they, together with the person Vega was replacing, would be leaving immediately on an extended road trip. Over the next ten days, the three men visited dozens of the company's stores all over Spain. Finally, they pulled up in front of a Zara store in Madrid. The CEO turned to Vega and said, "This is where you will be working."

Caught by surprise, Vega responded, "But I have never managed a retail store before!"

"That's OK," the CEO replied. "You won't be managing the store. You will be a sales associate."

The CEO introduced Vega to the store manager. After a brief welcome, the manager turned to Vega and said, "Let me introduce you to your new boss."

The new boss turned out to be a twenty-year old girl with bright dyed-red hair and a large number of body piercings.

Vega turned to the CEO and asked, "How long will I be working here?"

The CEO shrugged, "I have no idea."

"Does Ortega know about this?" Vega asked.

"It was his idea."

Recounting this story to us years later, Vega said "My stint as a sales associate was the most effective development experience I have ever had. It made me humble. It was also the beginning of a life experience with Zara that completely changed the way I thought about how to run a business."

While humility is a prerequisite for managing in an idea-driven manner, other characteristics are necessary as well. These include being improvement oriented and execution minded, and having the ability to work well collaboratively. When Pete Wilson, CEO of Pyromation, an Indiana thermocouple manufacturer with 120 employees (averaging 45 implemented ideas per person per year or so), began transforming his company, he brought in a consultant with a PhD in organizational behavior to help his top managers make the transition to the idea-driven leadership style he was looking for. Early on, two of his top managers didn't like the changes being made and left. Wilson hired an executive search firm to help create an in-depth profile of the type of people he wanted on his leadership team. This profile was used to develop a detailed questionnaire to guide the process of evaluating prospects and, once hired, to structure their ongoing development.

The characteristics of idea-driven leaders are similar to those of the "Level 5" leaders that Jim Collins found in his best-selling *Good to Great* study.[8] Level 5 leaders, the ones who successfully led their companies' transition to greatness, were humble people who put their organizations first and were determined to improve them. While Collins found such people to be rare in top leadership positions, Jay Reardon of Hickory Chair insisted that they are plentiful, but the place to look for them is three or four tiers down in the organization's hierarchy—exactly where the Luthans study predicts managers more concerned with being effective than being promoted will be predominantly found.

The problem is that the people in the best positions to identify such leaders are usually their subordinates. Subordinates know the true characters of their bosses and whether they are truly improvement oriented and responsive to ideas. This is why a 360-degree review process, like the one initiated by General Dempsey, holds the promise of providing much better evaluations of managers than can be done by their superiors alone. However, while the 360-degree review is an attractive concept, a note of caution is needed. The process is difficult to get right and rarely delivers fully on its promise. Unless the right conditions are set by the leaders, and subordinates have a great deal of trust in the confidentiality of the process, they will not provide honest feedback. It is dangerous and foolish for subordinates to point out their bosses' weaknesses in an unsecure process, particularly as their comments will be documented and remain in the organization's files for a long time.

Changing Management Mindsets and Behaviors

When Wilf Blackburn took over as CEO of Ayudhya Allianz, the Thai subsidiary of Munich-based insurance giant Allianz, the company was run in a heavily top-down manner and was a minor player in the Thai market. His first actions were to set up an idea system, educate his managers and employees in what would be expected of them, and begin identifying and eliminating the barriers that impeded the flow of ideas.

Blackburn abolished the company's dress code, knocked down walls— literally—and eliminated high-walled cubicles to open up the offices and improve interdepartmental communication. He relocated managers nearer to their subordinates, scheduled quarterly idea fairs around the company to showcase ideas, and instituted a spectacular off-site annual idea celebration and recognition event for everyone in the company. He also had his managers select the themes for the quarterly idea campaigns so the resulting ideas would help them with their unit's goals, and he incorporated each manager's idea management performance into his formal performance reviews.

Within three years Ayudhya Allianz won a Stevie award for being one of the most innovative companies in Asia, and Blackburn himself was named Best Executive in Asia (subcontinent, Australia and New Zealand) in the International Business Awards. The company was also named the most innovative of the 120 "operating enterprises" in the global Allianz family.

And by the end of Blackburn's fourth year, Ayudhya Allianz had moved from twenty-fourth in revenue among Thai insurance companies to second, and it was *first* in terms of new policies underwritten (i.e., growth rate).

Blackburn was already an experienced change agent when he assumed control of Ayudhya Allianz. The effectiveness of his actions is perhaps best explained by viewing them from the perspective of change theory. In their landmark study of hundreds of different approaches to changing a person's behavior, Kenneth Benne and Robert Chin separated them into three categories: the *rational-empirical* (using data and logic), the *normative–re-educative* (educating people to look at things differently), and the *power-coercive* (forcing conformance).[9] Collectively, Blackburn's actions covered all three categories. His rational-empirical tactics were to show managers the benefits of ideas through idea fairs and engaging them in choosing idea campaign themes. His normative–re-educative tactics, all designed to get his managers to change their perspectives and ways of thinking, were manifested in the new training programs he created and in his tearing down walls, locating managers close to their charges, and promoting ideas through lavish celebrations. And, of course, holding his managers accountable for their idea management performance was a power-coercive approach.

Whatever the mix of tactics you choose to work on your managers' mindsets and behaviors, your efforts will have a much better chance of success if you use a synergistic balance of Benne and Chin's three dimensions of creating change. In the rest of this chapter, we describe some effective tactics in each area.

The Rational Approach: Building the Case for Ideas. One of the most common questions we are asked by people who are interested in starting an idea system in their organizations is how to convince (possibly reluctant) senior managers that it is worth doing. If senior managers have never been exposed to a high-performing idea system, they may find it difficult to imagine what one can do for their organization. Consequently, an effective first step is to expose senior managers to a sizeable quantity of good ideas from their own employees.

At Big Y World Class Market, one of the largest independently owned supermarket chains in New England, CEO Donald D'Amour came up with a very effective tactic to do just this for his leadership team. During the pilot stage of his idea system, he held monthly leadership meetings for the sole purpose of reviewing all the ideas submitted in the three pilot stores and assessing how they had been handled. Over the six-month pilot, the senior leaders looked at hundreds of implemented ideas. Even though most of them were small, it was clear that their cumulative impact was huge (a small sample of these ideas is given in Chapter 7). This process convinced the leadership team that an idea system would be an enormous help in meeting their company's goals. It forced them to engage with the new idea process and confront the changes they would need to make in management systems or policies that interfered with the flow of ideas. It also gave them a fresh appreciation of what was taking place on the front lines in their stores.

For example, one of the first ideas was from a woman in the deli department. It had to do with the numbered tickets that customers pulled from a dispenser to get their place in line for service. The problem was that when she finished serving one customer, before turning to the next, she had to walk twenty feet down to the end of the counter to hit the button to advance the overhead sign to the next customer's number. She pointed out that this meant that her first action as the next customer stepped forward was to turn her back and walk away, starting that person's service experience off on a negative note. Her idea was to put three buttons spaced along the deli counter so employees could conveniently press one while beginning to serve the next customer. D'Amour used this idea frequently in his meetings with directors across the company to show them how a very simple idea—one that was most readily seen by someone directly serving the customers—made the employees' jobs easier and more productive while improving customer service.

D'Amour was a champion of the idea system from the outset. He took on himself the task of winning over the other members of his leadership team. Although rare, such championing from the top certainly makes all the change involved a lot easier. More often the initial championing comes from midlevel managers with much less power. But they can still find ways to put large numbers of employee ideas in front of their senior leaders.

We recently watched a middle manager at a large European insurance company use this tactic with his superiors. The company had been using an electronic suggestion box that was averaging 0.2 ideas per person per year with an 8 percent implementation rate. Although the CEO dutifully attended the annual awards banquets and said all the right things, he was hardly a champion of employee ideas. Worse, at least half the company's leadership team was openly hostile to investing any effort whatsoever in eliciting employee ideas.

It was obvious that the idea system needed to be scrapped and a new one created. After some persuasion, the CEO gave this middle manager permission to develop and pilot a new process. Within two months, some of the six pilot areas were averaging more than one implemented idea per person per month—*750 times* more than before. The middle manager selected a sample of 30 ideas, listed them on a single "idea sheet" (much like Table 1.1), and met with the CEO and COO.

As he walked them through the ideas, their excitement mounted. Most of the ideas were small but were obvious improvements and easy to implement. Taken collectively, they clearly had a significant impact on performance. The two men could now envision the significant benefits of a company-wide idea system. At the CEO's request, over the next few days, the middle manager met with all members of the leadership team individually, showing them the idea sheet and letting them see its implications. Soon afterward, the CEO began championing employee ideas regularly in his talks around the company.

Reeducating Managers. Although some leaders can be convinced of the value of front-line ideas when exposed to a large number of them, such exposure alone is rarely enough for a person to overcome years of entrenched bad habits and to change his or her management style. A deeper intervention is needed, the nature and extent of which will vary depending on where the manager sits in the organization's hierarchy and exactly how much that person's behavior and attitude need to change.

For lower-tier managers, who are closer to the front lines, installing new idea processes combined with a day or two of thoughtfully designed training, followed by a short-term regime of coaching, is usually sufficient. But sometimes a little more help is needed. For example, during the pilot-testing of its new idea system, a U.K. financial services company was experiencing a huge variance in performance between the different pilot areas. While several supervisors were doing quite well, the majority were struggling. After looking into the reasons behind this variance, it appeared that the two dominant factors were (1) the supervisor's attitude toward front-line ideas and (2) the supervisor's skills in idea management, particularly in idea meeting facilitation, coaching team members, and problem solving. To address these areas, an in-house certification program for idea management was designed for supervisors. To become certified, candidates had to attend two day-long training seminars, work through two books on idea management, and pass two online examinations on these books. A minimum of three of their idea meetings (this process is explained in Chapter 5) had to be observed by trained idea coaches, who provided structured feedback and had to "sign off" on each candidate's ability to lead effective idea meetings. Certification was awarded only after the supervisor's team had implemented at least one hundred ideas.

Note how effectively this certification program addressed both factors that had been identified. First, the skills gap was addressed by training—training that was put to use immediately, then backed up with observation and coaching. The online examinations made sure that the managers had read the books and understood the material. And then there was the test of supervisors' idea management skills through their teams' actual performance—that is, the requirement for one hundred implemented ideas. This requirement also helped to address the second issue: the supervisor's attitude. By the time a supervisor's team implements one hundred ideas, the supervisor should have come to appreciate the value of front-line ideas, become comfortable working with them, developed the right habits to encourage and stimulate them, and created a successful team that uses the idea process effectively in its daily work. In short, the supervisor should have become a true believer.

Ironically, most of the skills a supervisor needs to effectively manage ideas are skills that any supervisor should have anyway: listening, coaching, communicating, facilitating meetings, and leading improvement activities. Unfortunately, in organizations where supervisors' jobs are to give orders and assure compliance with them, they can slide by without many of these skills. But in idea-driven organizations, any shortcoming in these skills will quickly become obvious, as it will be reflected in their team's idea performance.

It is much more challenging to transform the thinking of recalcitrant higher-level managers and executives who don't see the value in front-line ideas. They are generally successful people who have built careers around the very habits and thinking that now hold them and their organizations back, on top of which they are suffering from the debilitating effects of having power. Consequently, they are often less open to new leadership concepts, and a deeper intervention is necessary. One of the more effective methods, in our experience, is a guided reading course for the company's top leadership.[10]

A few years ago, a prestigious national laboratory was struggling and risked possible closure. As part of a plan to cut costs and increase performance, its director brought us in to help set up an idea system. During our assessment, a number of issues were identified that were also primary contributors to the laboratory's overall poor performance. Many of these issues ultimately stemmed from the lab's promotion practices. For decades, its scientists had been selected for promotion into management positions based on their scientific prowess rather than their management skills. A further complication was that the leadership team members had a very low opinion of management as a profession, and they saw management training as silly and shallow. But they were open to a guided reading course, based on serious management books, which would give them the opportunity to explore new thinking and discuss how it might help to address some of the lab's substantive issues.

The first book, *Good to Great,* was selected partially because we felt the leadership team members (all scientists and engineers) would respect author Jim Collins's data-driven approach to discovering the elements needed to transform a good organization into a great one.

One of these elements, for example, is the importance of "confronting the brutal facts." An early homework question was "What are the most important brutal facts this leadership team is not confronting?" When the replies came back, they collectively identified that the lab's hiring and promotion processes focused on the wrong skills, and no one at any level was being held accountable for his or her performance.

Another of the book's main points was the importance of defining a simple and clear focus for the organization—the so-called hedgehog concept—and then to ruthlessly *stop doing* anything that was not within this focus. After considerable debate, the leadership team realized that the laboratory was not even close to having such a focus. Over the decades, it had grown haphazardly as disparate opportunities arose, and resources were now being dissipated across a host of unrelated programs and institutes.

In total, the leadership team studied seven books over a six-month period. By the end, the change in mindset of its members was profound, and they became a much more effective team. Among other things, they completely overhauled the HR process, developed a hedgehog concept that helped them prioritize projects, and set up an idea system.

When properly designed and used in the right context, reading courses can be highly effective. They can be customized to address the exact changes that are sought, and the pedagogy respects the complexity of leadership, the sophistication and judgment of the participants, and the need for them to discuss and debate how the concepts apply to their organizations. The readings and robust dialogue also create the common understanding and vocabulary that is a prerequisite for better teamwork.

However, reading courses are not risk-free for the participants. With the quality of each executive's thinking on display to colleagues and superiors, inflexibility and poor thinking are quickly exposed. The discussions also bring out areas of fundamental disagreement between managers. A skilled moderator can be important to minimize excessive conflict and draw out the key lessons.

Keeping managers in touch with the front lines. Even when managers believe that their people have good ideas and can be counted on to make good decisions about them, with all the power-related situational forces working to distance them from the front lines, their conviction will need ongoing reinforcement. This is one of the reasons that leaders of idea-driven organizations develop mechanisms to keep their busy managers engaged with front-line people and their ideas:

- John Boardman, the CEO who led Dubal (an aluminum producer in Dubai with three thousand employees) to become one of the most idea-driven companies in the Middle East, developed a recognition process designed to regularly expose his managers to large numbers of excellent front-line ideas. Annually, first-, second- and third-place awards were given for the best ideas in more than a dozen categories. Each department was expected to nominate one idea in each applicable category. The clever part of Boardman's scheme was the composition of the judging teams. Every upper manager, including Boardman himself, served on at least one team. To evaluate the ideas, the teams had to visit each department to hear presentations from the people whose ideas had been nominated and to see the results of these ideas firsthand.

- Toyota has long been an idea-driven organization. One of its core management concepts is the importance of managers at all levels regularly "going to *gemba*" to stay in touch with what is going on there. *Gemba* is Japanese for the actual place where the real work is done (i.e., the front lines). At Toyota, managers and employees are taught that everything that really matters happens at *gemba*.

- ThedaCare, an idea-driven health care system in Wisconsin, is widely recognized for the superior clinical results it delivers at costs significantly lower than the industry average. Every manager, even the CEO, must spend several hours each week at *gemba* as part of his "leader standard work," learning about issues, listening to ideas, and coaching. A concept from lean, leader standard work generally refers to a checklist of regular tasks that leaders must do to support improvement activities.

The value of keeping managers engaged with the front lines is greater than simply making them supportive of front-line ideas. It also helps them make much more informed decisions on major issues. Consider the following example from ThedaCare.

ThedaCare holds its Thursday morning leadership team meetings at a different one of its hospitals or clinics each week. Immediately following each meeting, the senior leaders each take a *gemba* walk in a different part of the facility. After one meeting held at the ThedaCare Clark Hospital, CEO John Toussaint decided to take his walk through the intensive care unit (ICU). He approached a nurse and asked if he could shadow her for about half an hour as she went about her work. She was happy to oblige.

The nurse's first stop was the room of an automobile accident victim. The patient was still unconscious, and three worried family members were huddling in a corner of the small room trying to stay out of the way as the nurse went about her work. Toussaint watched as the nurse had to go around the bed, twist and lean awkwardly over a shelf to adjust the patient's oxygen, and then a little while later do it again to check the suction tubes that were keeping the patient's airways clear. Both control and connection panels were attached to the wall in unwieldy positions. And while working with this awkward setup, she had to be careful to work around the IV pole, lines, and pumps.

Toussaint quickly realized that the ICU rooms were very poorly designed for modern medical care. They had been built many years before and were far too small to provide efficient care using modern technologies and methods. In addition, the movements the nurses needed to go through because of the space constraints and poor layout meant they could easily be injured. Furthermore, there was not enough room for family and visitors, who were important for the patients' morale and comfort.

Ironically, at that morning's leadership team meeting a $90 million renovation and construction project for the ThedaCare Hospitals had been discussed. Toussaint was about to take the proposal to the board of directors for approval. The project involved a major redesign of the facilities as part of a new "collaborative care" initiative. The pilot of this program had demonstrated significant improvements in the quality of health care delivered, and at a much lower cost. But the ICU, which was not directly related to the collaborative care delivery model, had been cut from the project. Immediately after leaving the ICU, Toussaint called ThedaCare's president and asked her why the ICU was not included in the proposal. The answer was for budget reasons—it would add $4 million to the proposal. But after a short discussion, they both agreed to add the $4 million for a new ICU back into the proposal. There was little difference, after all, between borrowing $90 million and $94 million.

In the end, the new rooms were more than double the size of the old ones, and they were designed to support the clinical process redesign as well as integrate the latest technologies in ways that made the work of the staff much easier and more efficient. Special lifts attached to the ceilings reduced injuries when transferring patients in and out of bed. Cabinets were installed so that regularly needed supplies could be stored in the rooms and resupplied by dedicated support functions on daily rounds, and medications could be delivered directly to the rooms where they would be used rather than to the nursing station. The rooms also had extra-wide doors and enough space to wheel in special equipment so a number of common tests and procedures—such as ultrasounds, electrocardiograms, and endoscopy—could be conducted right in the rooms rather than requiring patients in critical condition to be moved to other parts of the hospital.

The new rooms resulted in a significant improvement in productivity and increases in both patient and family satisfaction. In addition, the hospital was no longer requiring its front-line people to work in ways that could easily cause them injury. All this started with Toussaint shadowing a nurse on his weekly visit to the front lines.

As Key Fujimura, director of Continuous Improvement and Quality at Crane & Co., the high-end paper maker, once said to us, "When you go down to the front lines to see for yourself, you can use all five senses to decide if ideas are any good."

Unfortunately, many top-level managers make their decisions primarily on the financial numbers. As UCLA professor Theodore Porter wrote in his 1995 book *Trust in Numbers,* numbers are the language of distance. The problem with a myopic focus on numbers is that it shuts out the richness of the knowledge that comes from the front lines. "What is the financial return on that idea?" is often not the smartest question to ask. While cost-benefit analysis (CBA) is certainly useful, it deals with only part of the story—and often not the most important part.

A National Academy of Sciences study found that while CBA can accurately predict the effect of simple decisions, it is a poor technique for more complex ones, particularly for those with intangible and unpredictable elements.[11] Even its inventor, the French engineer-economist Jean Dupuit, warned of the limitations of CBA in his classic 1844 paper.[12] He cautioned that it would be easy for decision makers to take the numbers as gospel and not think past them. Because of these limitations, Dupuit stressed, CBA should be used to *inform* decisions, not to make them.

Applying Power: Accountability for Idea Performance. If an organization wants its managers to encourage and implement large numbers of frontline ideas, it needs to hold them accountable for doing so, just as it would for any other aspect of their performance. This can be done in a variety of ways, ranging from light social pressure to complete integration of idea performance into the organization's performance appraisal processes.

One of the lighter forms of accountability is transparency. When managers' idea performance is public and can be compared with their peers, and they know their bosses are watching, they will start paying more attention to ideas. A number of years ago, during a visit to a division of Air France, one of the authors noticed that one of a handful of graphs displayed in its lobby showed the number of implemented ideas in each of the division's eight units for the previous quarter. There was considerable disparity in the height of the bars, and each bar had the unit manager's name underneath it. The author asked the managing director what was done with this information. "Nothing," he replied. "You have to understand that it is impossible to become a senior manager without being very sensitive to what your boss is thinking. Just the fact that I have posted this data means that the situation will be totally different next year."

Transparency can also be used to hold managers accountable to their *subordinates* when it comes to following through on ideas. We found a good example of this at Scania, the Swedish truck maker, where ideas escalated from front line idea boards are posted on higher-level boards for managers to work on. All the boards, up to and including the leadership team's, are public so that everyone can easily see the progress of escalated ideas. This idea-by-idea transparency gives managers a powerful inducement to follow through on the ideas that come to them. Their employees are watching! (We will discuss the Scania system more in Chapter 5.)

Transparency alone, of course, does not create full accountability. For this, managers who do not do well at getting ideas from their people should face consequences, and managers who do well should be recognized and rewarded.

A number of years ago, the new CEO of Siemens VDO created strong accountability for ideas in a relatively simple way. Early on, he met with his idea system manager and told him that he wanted at least *fifteen* implemented ideas per person throughout his global organization of forty-four thousand people. The idea system manager came up with a simple Pareto-type chart that displayed the idea performance of each of the ninety-five business units (an illustrative version with fewer and fictional locations is shown in Figure 2.1). This chart became one of the CEO's favorite tools when reviewing his business directors' performance. When showing it to us, the idea system manager pointed to the laggards in the bottom right of the graph and commented, "When the CEO gets this chart, you do *not* want to be one of the executives out here." Similar approaches are used in many idea-driven organizations. As we explain in Chapter 4, it is usually quite straightforward to integrate idea performance into an organization's

FIGURE 2.1   Idea performance by unit

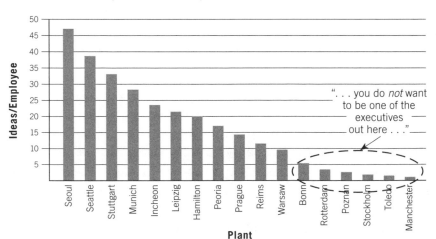

regular performance review process and to incorporate it into the criteria used for promotions, raises, and bonuses.

The most draconian type of accountability we have ever seen was in the late 1980s at Sumitomo Electric in Japan. At the time, the company was averaging some fifteen ideas per person. The CEO's policy was that any manager—from supervisor to vice president—who did not average at least five ideas per person in his area was ineligible for a raise or promotion for *three years*.

An idea-driven organization cannot be created or maintained without being led by the right kind of people. But the leaders themselves can only be as good as the structures and systems they set up to govern the way their organizations work. What we turn to next is how to modify these structures and systems so they enable the organization to be idea driven.

KEY POINTS

✓ As managers rise up the hierarchy and gain power, a host of situational forces come to bear on them that reduce their openness to ideas from subordinates. For example, research shows the following:

   ☐ Power reduces the complexity of a person's thinking and his or her ability to consider alternatives.

   ☐ People with power listen less carefully and have difficulty taking into account what others already know.

   ☐ People with power are less accurate in their estimates of the interests and positions of others, and they are less open to others' perspectives.

✓ Fighting the negative effects of power takes place on two fronts: (1) how managers are selected, developed, and promoted and (2) keeping managers grounded in what is happening on the front lines.

✓ Idea-driven organizations look for managers with humility when hiring and promoting, and they constantly cultivate it in their managers.

✓ Most of the skills a supervisor needs to effectively manage ideas are skills that any supervisor should have anyway: listening, coaching, communicating, facilitating meetings, and leading improvement activities. But in idea-driven organizations, any shortcomings in these skills quickly become obvious.

✓ Idea-driven organizations develop mechanisms to keep their busy managers engaged with front-line people and their ideas.

✓ "What is the financial return of that idea?" is often not the smartest question to ask. While numbers are certainly important, they tell only part of the story—and often not the most important part. Cost-benefit analysis (CBA) should be used to *inform* decisions, not to *make* them.

✓ Idea-driven organizations have mechanisms to hold managers accountable for encouraging and implementing large numbers of front-line ideas, just as they do for any other aspect of their performance.

3

Aligning the Organization to Be Idea Driven:

Strategy, Structure, and Goals

SEVERAL YEARS AGO, we helped a national chain of specialty stores to start an idea system. The company had been growing rapidly, doubling in size over the previous five years. But the CEO was concerned that it had also become bureaucratic and inflexible, and was losing its entrepreneurial energy and innovativeness. He believed that setting up a high-performance idea system would be a good way to start reinvigorating his organization.

Our assessment confirmed his opinion. The organization was indeed rife with constricting rules and policies that made it painful to implement even the smallest improvements. For example, a senior vice president (one of the top eight people in the company) told us that he had asked the information technology (IT) department for a set of speakers for his computer so that he could participate in an online webinar. Despite numerous reminders and follow-up phone calls, the speakers never arrived. It turned out that speakers were not part of the specified computer package for senior vice presidents. The vice president ended up having to bring in the speakers from his home computer.

This was not an isolated example. The company had created an infrastructure of tight controls that made it difficult to get anything done and would be a significant barrier to front-line ideas. For example:

- The purchasing process was extremely cumbersome. Even small purchases required a series of signatures (often including a senior vice president's), several price comparisons, and supporting documentation.
- Minor changes in the company's software, even when they would have significantly enhanced productivity, required the completion of extensive forms that justified the proposed changes and meetings with IT managers to negotiate the specifics of each change. Then funding for the programming time had to be obtained through a formal budget request process.
- Staffing levels in some departments were set daily at slightly below what the work standards projected would be needed for that day's volume of sales. The intent was to maximize productivity by having every minute of every front-line worker's day committed to regular work. Given this practice, it was very difficult for supervisors to free up time for their employees to work on developing and implementing ideas.
- The slightest change in a work procedure required extensive management review and had to be signed off by a director or vice president.

When we pointed out these and other issues to the CEO and his management team, we were surprised by their reaction. While they had long recognized the problems created by such tight controls, they were reluctant to loosen them. About eight years earlier, when the company was much smaller, its single-minded pursuit of rapid growth had led to chaos and inefficiency. To counter the resulting financial hemorrhaging, the leadership team had been forced to install draconian top-down controls that many of them believed had saved the company. Careful negotiations with top management were required to get temporary waivers from some of the more burdensome rules so that the pilot idea system could demonstrate the potential of a companywide system.

The three-month pilot, conducted in four key departments, was a resounding success. Three of the four departments averaged more than two implemented ideas per person per month, and the performance of all four improved significantly. Had the CEO not been willing to make the changes that were needed to remove critical barriers blocking the development and implementation of ideas in his organization, his idea system would not have been very successful.

A critical inflexion point occurs when a leader realizes that becoming idea driven involves a lot more than simply layering a mechanism to collect front-line ideas onto an existing organization. A host of additional changes need to be made as well. We have watched many leaders wrestle with the decision of whether to move forward. It is a big decision. They are essentially deciding whether they have the courage, energy, and even the ability to create an entirely different kind of organization, and whether their organization is ready for such substantial change. If management truly wants front-line ideas, it has to realign the organization to be idea driven. It has to create a culture where front-line ideas are valued and build management systems that are aligned to actively support their generation and implementation.

Figure 3.1 gives the framework that we use to conceptualize this alignment. Although we included this framework in *Ideas Are Free,* we are covering it in more detail here because we have learned that realignment plays a much bigger role in building an idea-driven organization than we initially thought. An organization faces a certain external *environment.* The *strategy* it follows must successfully draw needed resources from that environment. The organization's *structure* should be designed to support the strategy, as should the *policies* it follows and the way it *budgets* its resources. The *systems* and *procedures* it deploys, in turn, should be consistent with its strategy, structure, budgets, and policies. Smoothly meshing with all this is the way people are *rewarded,* the *skills* they are given through training, and the way they are *supervised.* The ultimate goal is to assure that throughout the organization, individual *behavior* is in line with the organization's strategic direction. The role played by the organization's *culture* and its *leadership* is to keep all these elements aligned. If

FIGURE 3.1 A framework for alignment

the strategy involves being idea driven, then all of these elements have to be aligned for ideas as well.

Ideas are voluntary. If people don't feel that their ideas will be welcomed and acted on rapidly and with a minimum of fuss, they can always keep the ideas to themselves, if they even think of them in the first place. This is why the flow of ideas is very sensitive to alignment. Although alignment is conceptually simple, in practice, it is very challenging to get right, and few organizations do it well.

For an organization to be well aligned for ideas, many different elements have to work together. Even one critical element out of alignment can make implementing an individual idea challenging or even block it. Neglect of just a few elements can undermine an entire idea system. In far too many organizations, ideas are forced to run a gauntlet of misaligned elements that is often unsurvivable.

In the remainder of this chapter and in Chapter 4, we discuss how to realign an organization to promote the flow of bottom-up ideas. This chapter focuses on the alignment of organizational structure and goals; Chapter 4 discusses the organization's management systems—the policies, procedures, and practices used to run it on a daily basis.

STRATEGY AND GOAL ALIGNMENT

Organizational structures come in a wide variety of forms—from traditional functional hierarchies to more contemporary process-based structures—but all of them have both *vertical* and *horizontal* elements. The vertical elements align top-level goals with the actions being taken at every level of the organization, while the horizontal elements assure that the different branches of the organization work well together. In this section we discuss how to align both elements in order to ensure that the ideas coming from the front lines are focused on helping the organization to achieve its strategic goals and improve its overall performance.

Vertical Alignment

While every manager knows that vertical alignment is critical, many leaders assume that their pro forma processes of cascading goals down their organizations are much more effective than they actually are. Sometimes, their goals don't even make it *one* level down, to the people they work with most closely.

Take, for example, what happened at an electronics retail chain in Spain and Portugal. The CEO, who had started an idea initiative a year earlier, asked us in because he felt the effort had stalled. The ideas that were being received were light and scattershot. We began by spending several days studying the idea system, visiting stores, interviewing employees and managers, and looking through the ideas that had come in.

The CEO's concern proved to be well founded: the ideas were indeed all over the map, on every topic under the sun, and many were of little value. Both managers and employees were frustrated with the idea system as they struggled with such basic questions as "What constitutes an idea?" or "Do changes as small as moving a wastebasket or rearranging a store display count as ideas?"

When presenting our findings to the company's leadership team, we explained that one of the main reasons the system was getting such poor ideas was that the corporate goals had not been effectively rolled down and internalized by front-line staff. As a result, many of the ideas that came in lacked focus and were only marginally helpful. Upon grasping the signifi-cance of this point, the CEO immediately turned to his leadership team and said, "I want each of you to make sure that your people have good metrics and understand what our goals are."

"Are you sure everyone in your leadership team understands what your company's goals are?" we asked.

"Of course they do!" the CEO shot back.

This view was inconsistent with what we had found, so we asked everyone on the leadership team, including the CEO, to write down on an index card what he or she considered to be the top three strategic goals for the company.

One of us then stepped out of the room, compiled the managers' stated goals, and created a chart comparing these with the CEO's. The results were eye-opening. None of the three goals that were most frequently cited by the company's top managers matched any of the CEO's three top goals! He had assumed that he had made his priorities clear to the entire organi-zation, but even his direct reports were hazy about them.

Ever since Robert Kaplan and David Norton popularized the notion of key performance indicators (KPIs)—specific measures of performance tied to goals—in their 1996 book *The Balanced Scorecard: Translating Strategy into Action,* many leaders have put increased emphasis on formally cas-cading goals and metrics down through their organizations. In practice, however, KPIs are generally used for deploying strategies and holding managers accountable for their performance rather than for encouraging front-line ideas that drive performance in a specific direction. Care is not always taken to translate top-level goals, as they are cascaded down, into metrics that front-line people can meaningfully affect through their ideas. Strategic goals such as "Increase market share to 8 percent" or "Lower operating costs to 40 percent of net revenue" have little meaning at the front-line level. Goals and measures must be properly *disaggregated* as they are passed down and then articulated in ways that front-line people can affect with their ideas.

We were able to demonstrate the power of properly translated goals to the CEO of that electronics retailer with an example from his own company. It turned out that the manager of the central warehouse had understood the CEO's goals—which were *high productivity, excellent customer service,* and *efficient use of capital*—and had translated them into metrics that his warehouse workers could understand and affect with their ideas:

- Shipments per week per employee (*productivity*),
- Percentage of orders shipped same day and correctly (*customer service*), and
- Inventory turnover (*use of capital*).

The manager posted the performance on these metrics on a weekly basis as a way to focus his team's ideas. Besides, he pointed out, keeping score added a bit of challenge and fun.

Because of these clear goals, his employees had implemented hundreds of small ideas that had dramatically improved the warehouse's performance. For example, at one point, the employees had been issued handheld scanners that wirelessly communicated with the central computer from anywhere in the warehouse. The original purpose of the scanners had been to ease the process of checking inventory in and out, by eliminating the need to use a scanner that was tethered to the terminal on the loading dock. But when the employees discovered the scanners were programmable, they came up with many ideas to increase the scanners' capability. Now, they can be used, from anywhere in the warehouse, to change inventory locations in the system and to instantaneously display the contents of a box, a shelf, or even an entire bay by simply scanning its bar code. The employees also programmed the scanners to display optimal order-picking routes for each order.

As a result of all these ideas, in just one year the warehouse was able to double the number of orders it shipped without adding any employees, reduce the number of orders filled incorrectly or shipped late by over 90 percent, and increase inventory turnover by 30 percent. In addition, the time required to take monthly inventory was cut by over 80 percent.

This example hit home with the CEO, who now understood why the warehouse was both getting a lot of ideas and performing well. Smiling, he told us of an idea that had recently come to his attention illustrating the high level of trust that had developed between management and the warehouse team. The idea had also given the warehouse manager a chance to recognize his team's exceptional performance. An employee suggested mounting a large flat-screen TV in the warehouse tuned to the sports channel, so people could monitor games of their favorite teams and keep up with the latest football (soccer) scores. The problem was, the suggester admitted, that whenever there were important matches, workers (even nonsmoking ones) were taking long smoking breaks to sit outside and listen to car radios during critical periods in the games. Or, they would leave early to rush home to watch the games. He suggested that a large flat-screen television in a central location would actually save time and improve productivity by eliminating the need for employees to surreptitiously leave the building to check on scores. The CEO joked to us, "With this group, I only hope the TV screen was big enough!"

Leaders are accustomed to thinking about their organizational goals in broad terms. When passing these goals down, it is easy for them to miss the importance of translating them into terms that are meaningful to the people whose actions are necessary to achieve them. Recently, for example, the chancellor of a major U.S. public university was anticipating large budget cuts due to shortfalls in state tax revenues. He set up a special website and issued a call to tens of thousands of faculty, staff, and students. "We need to find ways to save money. Please send in any ideas you have to cut costs." In the end, he got less than a hundred ideas and implemented only a handful.

The poor chancellor never had a chance with this campaign. For one thing, at the university, "cost cutting" was historically code for laying people off or eliminating programs. His faculty and staff would never engage with an initiative framed in these terms. But had the chancellor engaged his unit heads in passing down and expressing his goals in terms that were actionable and meaningful for their people, his campaign might have had a very different outcome. Consider, for example, the athletics department. How could its staff intelligently reduce expenses? A person working in the equipment lockers in the gym might be baffled if asked for ways to save money but could think of a lot of ideas if asked how to save energy and water (he does the laundry, controls the lighting, and patrols the locker rooms and showers), how to save on supplies, or how to reduce the amount of lost or damaged equipment. Had the chancellor ensured this type of translation occurred across all campus units, his request would have been more meaningful to the university's staff and students, and he would have received a lot more useful money-saving ideas.

The effective translation of organization-level goals into lower-level goals requires the ability to identify key leverage points, as well as the creativity to frame them in an actionable way. One of the more memorable examples of this that we have seen occurred at Fresh AB, the Swedish ventilation products manufacturer. At the time, Fresh was confronting the need to make a major strategic shift in its markets. The company sold products in three different markets: home construction, commercial construction, and consumer retail (do-it-yourself). Economic forecasts projected a significant drop in new home construction. To compensate for the expected sales drop in this market, the leadership team wanted to increase sales in the consumer retail market. The retail sales channels included hardware and home improvement stores, particularly the increasing number of "big box" retailers.

Rather than simply assigning the sales and marketing staff the "stretch goal" of doubling retail sales, Fresh's leadership team took a different approach. Since retail display space is the primary driver of retail sales, it translated its high-level goal into one that everyone could contribute ideas toward achieving: *Double the number of product displays in retail stores.* If the goal had remained to double sales, it would have most likely been interpreted as "sales and marketing need to work harder." Few people outside the sales and marketing departments would have offered meaningful ideas. But everyone could help with the display goal.

Ideas came in for more attractive packaging, enhanced display designs, displays of different sizes and configurations to better fit the needs of more retailers, eye-catching new products and color schemes, and a variety of other display-related improvements. As a result, Fresh was able to reach its retail sales expansion goal before the decline in new home construction, an impressive accomplishment that would probably have been impossible for sales and marketing to pull off alone.

Another dimension that leaders have to consider when setting goals is whether the goals are in the interests of the people who are expected to work toward them. If not, no matter how well they are articulated, few ideas will be offered. Take, for example, what happened at a Silicon Valley company that was part of a major global engineering corporation with almost a hundred business units. Shortly before our visit, this company had won the award for the best idea system in the entire corporation. Senior managers, several of whom had just returned from the award ceremony in Europe, were justifiably proud of their idea system, which had saved millions of dollars in the previous year. We reviewed the ideas this unit had received during its winning year and interviewed the groups and individuals that had been the most prolific idea generators. Some of the ideas were very creative and had saved considerable sums of money. We were particularly impressed by the company's success with employee ideas given its recent history.

Before being purchased as a strategic acquisition by its current corporate parent, it had been a rapidly growing high-technology startup that had developed some very innovative and high-margin products. Its primary focus had been on breakthrough technology and sophisticated product engineering. Production costs had never been a priority for the company, as they had been a relatively small part of its overall cost structure. Its manufacturing operations were quite inefficient, and the new corporate parent had begun systematically shifting production offshore and had already laid off more than two-thirds of its manufacturing workforce. The message was clear. The facility had to lower its production costs further or eventually it would be reduced to only a research center. So management turned to its employees for cost-saving and productivity-enhancing ideas. At first glance, the award-winning system appeared to be a resounding success. However, management never realized what it was missing.

As we went through the ideas, a pattern began to emerge. All of the ideas involved ways to save material, shipping costs, or other non-personnel-related expenses. *None* of them involved working more efficiently. Yet the production floor was rife with obvious labor-saving improvement opportunities. This was puzzling until we realized that with the company steadily cutting its production workforce, ideas that saved labor would quickly result in the elimination of more jobs. Discrete conversations with several employees and front-line supervisors revealed that they were indeed focusing on cost-savings ideas that did not impact labor.

Having already seen enough of their friends lose their jobs, they were not about to offer ideas that would justify any more layoffs.

The threat of layoffs does create a special dynamic when it comes to front-line ideas. Why would anyone offer ideas if it could cost them or their colleagues their jobs? Generally, idea-driven organizations do whatever they can to avoid layoffs and, in many cases, even offer some form of job security with respect to performance improvement coming from ideas. They do this because they understand the importance of front-line ideas and don't want to cut them off. They are able to do it because the ideas they get put them in better positions than their traditionally run counterparts to respond effectively to market shocks or downturns, as they are generally more flexible and perform at much higher levels.

Horizontal Alignment

When a small East Coast specialty insurance company started an idea system, one of the early ideas came from a customer service representative who suggested an improvement to the company's customer management software. Every time she finished talking with one customer, she had to exit the application and restart it in order to access the next customer's data. Why not create the ability to switch between customers without exiting the software? When her colleagues discussed her idea, they unanimously agreed that it should be quickly implemented. They estimated that the problem wasted seven minutes of each of the thirty representative's time every day, or 3.5 hours total, the equivalent of almost half a person. Moreover, the service delays irritated customers who had to wait while their information was being pulled up. But when the idea arrived at the IT department, because it would take three to four hours of a programmer's time to implement, it was rejected. This was a classic example of horizontal misalignment.

The IT department had been tasked with three things: running the help desk, maintaining current systems, and working on large strategic software initiatives. Implementing front-line ideas was not part of its charge. Furthermore, it was under pressure to keep its costs down, and the time to implement this idea would come out of its budget.

The manager of IT was acting rationally according to his assigned goals. From the perspective of the company as a whole, however, it was silly not to implement the idea. The small sacrifice that the IT department was being asked to make—three to four hours of work, only once—was far outweighed by the improvement it would have created in the customer service department—three to four hours saved *every day*.

Horizontal goal misalignment is extremely prevalent. When setting goals, many leaders focus on rolling down their goals and put little thought into whether these might conflict at lower levels. And when the symptoms of horizontal misalignment emerge, they are usually attributed to other causes, such as personality conflicts between managers, territoriality, excessive personal ambition, or some other human failing. So it goes undiagnosed.

Horizontal misalignment is often rooted in the way organizations are structured. The most popular configuration is by *function*—that is, marketing, accounting, operations, and so on. Each of these functions, in turn, is broken down into more and more finely segmented tasks, until the department or team level is reached. But since the organization's processes cut across these segmented tasks, many ideas that improve these processes will have cross-departmental implications. Unless great care is taken with how department-level goals are designed, many departments will end up with goals that can most easily be met at the expense of other departments or the process as a whole.

Horizontal misalignment is also costly. The following example demonstrates how the very same idea that *failed* after several years of trying it in a horizontally misaligned organization was quickly and successfully implemented in an idea-driven one. It offers a rare chance to quantify some of the costs of such misalignment.

A number of years ago, a global aerospace company bought a large automated storage and retrieval system for its spare parts inventory. The $2.5 million system included computer-controlled robotic technology that could store and retrieve tens of thousands of parts in more than 5,400 bins. The problems started once the system was physically installed and ready to be programmed. The IT and inventory control departments fought over who would do the programming and the system became the object of a turf war. Caught in the middle, the front-line workers operating it had to manually record the locations of parts in a spiral-bound notebook as they were moved in and out of the huge storage system. This notebook was stolen once and had to be re-created by painstakingly retrieving each of the 5,400 bins and logging its contents—some *two weeks* of wasted labor for six people. Moreover, the manual process of logging parts as they were loaded into and extracted from the system led to human errors. Sometimes a part was called for and was not in its documented location—it was lost somewhere in the system. Whenever this happened, the operators would have to go through the bins one by one until they found the missing part. Eventually, the problems with the system led the aerospace company to abandon it entirely and put it up for auction on the Internet.

What was particularly interesting was *who* ended up buying the system and *how*. Task Force Tips (TFT) is a medium-sized manufacturer of firefighting equipment headquartered in Indiana. In 2009, the growing company was moving to a larger facility. The plan was to maintain full production while gradually shifting it to the new facility over a three-month period. One of the last items scheduled to be moved was the old automated inventory storage and retrieval system. Moving this equipment would be time-consuming—it was heavy; had four bays that were each sixteen feet high, four feet wide, and forty feet long; and contained five hundred storage bins plus robotic lifting equipment. Until this storage system could be moved, TFT planned to purchase simple racks to temporarily store parts at the new location and handle the inventory there manually.

The engineer assigned to locate a company that could fabricate the temporary racks was shocked at their high cost. But he had an idea. Maybe, he thought, the company could buy another (and bigger) automated storage and retrieval system for not too much more money than the temporary racks would cost. This approach would simplify the move and also help with the company's increasing need for storage. The current storage system was already nearing its capacity. It was also wearing out. The idea was quickly escalated to CEO Stewart McMillan, who told the engineer that he had a better chance of being struck by lightning than being able to find such a system for a price that would make it worthwhile, but the engineer looked into the idea anyway.

Searching on the Internet, the engineer found the aerospace firm's storage system for sale and noticed that it would be auctioned on the Internet in just a few days. It was ideal for TFT's needs. It was practically new and had twice the storage capacity of the company's old system. When McMillan was informed, he invited the engineer and some others to his house for a "bid-watching party." Early on, the group decided to submit the minimum bid of $1,000, fully expecting to be quickly outbid. But no further bids came in. With only minutes left, the group still expected to see a number of bidders jump in at the last minute. They were surprised when *no* bids did come in, and an e-mail arrived informing them that they had won. While the system was practically free, it had to be disassembled, shipped halfway across the country (in *twenty-seven* truckloads), and reassembled. In the end, TFT got the system up and running for only $600,000.

Think about what this story illustrates. The misalignment between IT and inventory control at the aerospace company rendered a $3.5 million investment ($2.5 million for equipment and $1 million for installation) *worthless*. On top of this loss was all the extra labor wasted on operating it manually, searching for all the lost parts, and infighting, as well as the inefficiencies that poor inventory control created throughout the company. It was interesting for us to watch a poorly aligned aerospace company being taken advantage of by a nimbler idea-driven company. Essentially, TFT was able to purchase and install a slightly used automated storage system for less than twenty cents on the dollar!

At first glance, the inability of the aerospace company to get the inventory system working properly, despite all of its resources, appeared to be the result of a political battle between the IT and inventory control departments. While we did not have the opportunity to directly investigate the underlying causes of the interdepartmental warring at this company, as we noted earlier, when departments or managers don't work well together, the behavior is usually rooted in some form of horizontal misalignment— such as conflicting goals or performance measures, inflexible budget rules, or poorly conceived bonus or promotion systems.

Seemingly logical approaches taken to hold people accountable, or to incentivize and reward them, often create, or significantly aggravate, horizontal misalignment. Take pay-for-performance, for example. Although it may seem sensible at the individual level, it often backfires dramatically at the organizational level by creating *disincentives* for people to work together. One of the larger retail chains in the United States created a bonus system that all but guaranteed that if a good idea came up in one store, it would *never* be shared with other stores. The chain was organized into regions, and store managers' bonuses were based on their store's performance ranking relative to the other stores in their region. The top-ranked manager got the largest bonus, the second-ranked one got the second-largest bonus, and so on down the line. One store manager told us that if he were to share a profitable idea with another store manager, he would essentially be cutting his own bonus. The competitive bonus system completely shut down the vital sharing and cooperation that should have been occurring between stores.

Creating Horizontal Linkages

Most work in organizations requires some form of interaction between different departments or units. But the complexity of all but the smallest and simplest organizations makes it impossible to establish individual unit goals that naturally assure that everyone will work together toward the common good. Some form of linkage mechanism is needed to tie the interests and actions of the various units together. This section discusses a number of these mechanisms.

A highly visual/spatial approach is to reconfigure the physical work space. Often, simply removing physical barriers and co-locating departments that have to work together greatly improves the level and quality of cooperation and interpersonal interactions, increases trust and understanding, and facilitates joint problem solving and ideas. It often has a considerable symbolic "shock" effect as well. Recall Wilf Blackburn, the turnaround specialist at Allianz discussed in Chapter 2. By the time we met him, he already had developed a reputation within Allianz for "blowing out walls" when he was put in charge of a unit, as he did at Ayudhya Allianz. We visited him in Shanghai just five months after he had been appointed CEO of Allianz China. When Blackburn took over, he was under pressure from headquarters to cut costs and increase profitability, and to do so rapidly. But instead of simply looking for things he could cut immediately, Blackburn *invested* considerable money in breaking down barriers and building his organization's flexibility and innovativeness. For him, this was one of his primary leverage points for transforming the company.

One of his first acts was to tear down the walls of his own office and replace them with floor-to-ceiling glass. Much as he would have liked a private office, he was sending a message to his organization: we will be transparent and collaborative in the way we work. A few weeks later, construction crews removed the physical walls between departments, and the high cubicle dividers were replaced by ones of waist height. This created enough new space to allow Blackburn to consolidate his two-building operation into one, further integrating his workforce while also saving money. Blackburn told us that his goal was to create a headquarters building with an open layout that encouraged people to communicate and work together, in order to create a more flexible, idea-driven company.

Another tactic that gets people to think in terms of the whole is to create an ambitious unifying vision for the entire organization—a "Big Hairy Audacious Goal," or "BHAG," as Jim Collins and Jerry Porras term it in their classic 1994 book *Built to Last: Successful Habits of Visionary Companies*. Subaru Indiana Automotive's quest for zero landfill, discussed more in Chapters 7 and 8, is a good example of such a goal. It excited everyone, and everyone could contribute to achieving it with their ideas and actions. The horizontal alignment created by this BHAG was critical because almost every green idea requires cross-departmental collaboration. Consider, for example, the many simple ideas that came in to return packaging material to various suppliers for reuse. Who needed to be involved? The ideas originated in operations from the people who unpacked the parts, but engineering was needed to certify that the materials could be reused, and purchasing had to negotiate with the suppliers, who needed to change their processes to take back and reuse the materials. There were also cost and price implications. Transportation and logistics had to get involved in handling, packaging, and shipping the materials back to the suppliers, and accounting had to deal with any budget and control ramifications. Unless *everyone* shared the green vision, progress on these ideas would have quickly bogged down.

Over the years, considerable thought has been put into how to get people to think beyond their own limited piece of an operation. Take, for example, the notion of "internal customers," popularized by the quality expert Joseph Juran in the late 1980s. The thinking was that each person (or group) in a larger process should identify his internal customers—the people immediately downstream in the process that received his output—and focus on the best ways to meet their needs. If everyone satisfies their internal customers, the quality delivered at the end of the chain should satisfy the final "external customers," too. The internal customer concept was a way to inject awareness of the larger process into people's thinking, and it is easy to adopt without making many additional changes in an organization or its structure. Its drawback is that it links units only with their immediate neighbors.

Performance bonuses, when properly designed, are another way to tie people directly to everyone else in a process. Nucor Steel uses a weekly bonus system, based on the previous week's output, to focus everyone's attention on the output of an entire steel mill. A worker's bonus, which can more than double his or her weekly pay, is not based on individual performance or even the performance of the group, but on the output of the entire process—the work of all shifts in all departments combined. In this way, people are rewarded not only for their performance but for how much their work helps the performance of other departments and the mill as a whole.

The approaches we have discussed so far are intended to create a common purpose by making people think in terms of the impact of their ideas on the entire process. But none of these approaches offer all the advantages of fully horizontal structures that directly integrate interrelated operations into a single stream.

One of the early champions of process thinking was Henry Ford. Breaking with the scientific management tradition of his era, which focused on maximizing the productivity of individual operations and reinforcing it through the use of piece rates, Ford optimized his entire process to achieve continuous flow. Half a century later, Toyota raised process thinking to a new level. Among other things, it introduced the concept of value-stream mapping, a tool that allowed its people to graphically illustrate the structure and performance of an entire supply chain. It allowed people to easily see where improvement efforts should be focused to enhance the process as a whole.

We often think back to a comment in 1989 by Shigeo Shingo, one of the developers of the Toyota Production System. He told us that he felt that most managers around the world were continuing to miss the significance of the difference between processes and individual operations, and this lack of understanding was one of the biggest things holding productivity down. Since that time, a lot has changed. Today, while more managers recognize the importance of process and are applying many improvement techniques that do focus on the process as a whole, they are still battling organizational structures fundamentally designed around individual operations rather than the process as a whole.

STRUCTURING FOR IDEAS

Up to this point, we have discussed how to overcome vertical and horizontal misalignment in organizations with more or less traditional structures. Such problems can be avoided in the first place by designing an organization specifically for the purpose of getting and rapidly implementing large numbers of ideas. A good example is Zara, the "fast-fashion" retailer discussed in the last chapter. In the fashion industry, it normally takes a year or more to create and deliver new clothing. At Zara, it takes less than fifteen days to create a new design and deliver the finished clothing to its thousands of stores around the world. Every aspect of the company is designed to promote speed, particularly speed in getting and acting on information and ideas.

Rather than using a conventional departmental structure that would group people doing given tasks according to their specializations, Zara organizes its development process around three-person teams: a designer, who does the actual design work; a commercial, who coordinates the material and production tasks; and a country manager, who coordinates the retail operations in a particular country. These teams are responsible for developing new clothing and shepherding it from concept through design, prototyping, manufacturing, and delivery. The company's design floor is the size of an aircraft hangar, with an open layout and no walls. One end of the floor has clusters of desks arranged by team, with the designers' CAD systems located nearby. Founder Amancio Ortega's desk is located here as well.

Another important component of Zara's business model is to make clothing in small batches of only three to four weeks of demand. This means that individual design decisions do not carry high stakes, so they can be made at the team level. New design ideas for clothing or accessories are shared among team members, and the teams make their decisions quickly—usually in just a few hours. It is striking how young these team members are—most are in their twenties or early thirties. This means the people making the design decisions match the demographics of the typical Zara customer. The result is more successful design choices and reduced risk.

Compare this process with that of a typical fashion clothing company, where designs are generated by designers who have branded themselves over years in the business. Final design and purchasing decisions, which involve orders for an entire season, are made by senior vice presidents. Then the clothes are made in large batches by manufacturers half a world away. It is not surprising that the typical design-to-retail cycle is a year or more.

While new design ideas at Zara come from a wide variety of sources, including the fashion runways of Milan, Paris, and New York, most come from Zara's front-line retail associates. Each country manager talks with every one of his or her store managers at least twice a week. The main topics of conversation are the observations made by the retail staff about which products are moving well, what the more fashionable customers are wearing, and what items are being requested that the store *does not* carry. For example, when employees in Northern European stores began reporting that the more fashionable customers were wearing higher boots, the message was quickly forwarded to the design teams in Spain. Both high boots and clothing that would complement them were quickly created and added to Zara's line.

Once a design is finalized by a team, it is sent from the team's CAD system to the prototyping area on the other side of the design floor. Within hours, samples are constructed on various sizes of manikins. Each team meets around the manikins, where any ideas for modifications or finishing touches are discussed and decided upon before the final version is sent to manufacturing. While most fashion companies source all their manufacturing from suppliers in low-labor-cost countries such as Vietnam, Bangladesh, or Sri Lanka—and Zara does this, too, for some of its staple clothing products—the company contracts all of its fast-fashion locally in northwest Spain for greater speed and flexibility. Finished clothing is shipped by truck to stores in Europe and by air to stores in the rest of the world.

Zara's competitive advantage is its ability to provide customers with the latest fashion in clothing at a reasonable price. To do this, it has to be able to tap large numbers of ideas from customers and staff, and act on them quickly. Remember from Chapter 2 that Ortega started his business out of frustration at his boss's unwillingness to listen. Everything about Zara is designed for ideas: the constitution of the design teams and the authority granted to them, the communication protocols with the stores, the physical layout of the design-to-prototyping facility, and the decision to source manufacturing locally.

This last point is significant. Managers at another fashion company we worked with told us that one of their biggest problems was that only one person spoke English at the Chinese factory where they sourced their product. Communication was difficult and highly error prone, and costly and time-consuming mistakes occurred every day. Zara's suppliers, in contrast, are close by—most are in the same community—and communications are clear and simple. Literally, nothing is lost in translation.

Structure and goal alignment are the *strategic* aspects of realignment. In the next chapter, we turn to the *operational* aspects—that is, how to align an organization's *management systems* for front-line ideas.

KEY POINTS

✓ Becoming idea driven involves more than simply layering an idea process onto an existing organization. The entire organization must be aligned to support the development and implementation of ideas.

✓ In far too many organizations, ideas are forced to run a gauntlet of misaligned elements that is often unsurvivable. While alignment is conceptually simple, in practice, it is challenging to get right, and very few organizations do it well.

✓ Many leaders assume that their pro forma processes of cascading goals down their organizations are much more effective than they actually are. When passing goals down, it is important to frame them in terms that are meaningful to and actionable by the people on the front lines.

✓ Horizontal goal misalignment is extremely prevalent and very costly. When setting goals, most leaders focus on rolling down their goals, with little thought about how these goals might conflict at lower levels.

✓ Most work in organizations requires some form of interaction between different departments or units. Idea-driven organizations create mechanisms to link the interests and actions of their various units together.

✓ Although many managers recognize the importance of taking a process-centric approach, they are still battling organizational structures fundamentally designed around individual operations rather than the process as a whole. Such problems can be avoided in the first place by designing an organization specifically for the purpose of getting and implementing large numbers of front-line ideas rapidly.

4

Aligning the Organization to Be Idea Driven: Management Systems

AN ORGANIZATION'S MANAGEMENT systems consist of all the processes and procedures used to govern the way it works, from the budgeting process and how people are rewarded, to the procedures used to make products and deliver services. Typically, management systems evolve incrementally over time in response to shifting needs for coordination and control, with little thought for their impact on the flow of ideas. Consequently, the management systems in most organizations are seriously misaligned for bottom-up ideas.

While many aspects of goal misalignment discussed in the last chapter can be corrected in a single planning cycle, fixing the elements discussed in this chapter is more of an ongoing effort. Management systems generally consist of many moving parts, all interacting with one another. The resulting complexity makes it impossible to ever resolve all misalignments completely, and new ones are created all the time. Even the best idea-driven organizations still find subtle misalignments after years of constant vigilance and ongoing effort to root them out.

In this chapter, we continue the march down the framework for alignment given in Figure 3.1, discussing how to realign each of the management systems in it for ideas.

BUDGETING AND RESOURCING THE IDEA PROCESS

We were once invited to help a division of a venerable Wall Street financial services company become more innovative. Its products and services were aging, its once-huge margins were eroding, and its leaders were concerned about the division's lack of new products. It had not introduced a single new product or service in more than ten years. As we interviewed managers and employees, a clear pattern emerged. In its attempts to maximize short-term profits, management had overloaded the staff. No one had time to work on anything new. When we pointed out to the leadership team that its overemphasis on *exploiting* existing products and services was undermining its people's ability to *explore* for new ones that would increase margins and drive the organization's future profits, its members were rattled. After considerable debate about the ramifications of this practice, the leadership team decided that margins were still good enough, and the company would continue to focus on exploiting existing products, rather than investing the valuable time of its skilled financial professionals in working on new products with uncertain futures. This decision was not surprising, given that senior managers' performance evaluations and bonuses were based on *current* profits.

Ideas are an investment in the future. As with any investment, resources need to be committed up front. A surprisingly large number of leaders sacrifice their organizations' futures by focusing too eagerly on current profits and failing to allocate the resources their people need to work on developing and implementing new ideas.

In this section, we address the three most common resourcing needs for bottom-up ideas: *time, money,* and *assistance from support functions.*

Resourcing for Time

People need time to develop and implement ideas. Finding this time for front-line employees, however, can be a real challenge, particularly at first.

Managers frequently ask how much time front-line employees should be given to work on ideas. We generally recommend that everyone should have a minimum of an hour and a half per week—a half an hour for their idea meeting, and another hour to develop or implement ideas (more on the mechanics of idea processes in the next chapter). It is hard to make progress at a satisfactory rate with anything less than this time allotment. Idea-driven organizations typically commit between 4 and 7 percent of their front-line employees' time for ideas. The most aggressive commitment of front-line time we have ever encountered was at Softwin, a Romanian software company best known for its BitDefender antivirus program. The company expected everyone to spend 25 percent of their time working on their own ideas.

When managers and supervisors first realize how much time their people will need to work on ideas, they often worry about where this time is going to come from. One tactic that is particularly helpful in this regard is to start out by asking employees to focus on time-saving ideas or ideas on non-value-adding tasks that their teams could stop doing. Almost every time we have seen this tactic used, the resulting ideas have quickly freed up more time per week than the teams needed to work on ideas. A typical example of this phenomenon occurred a few years ago at a call center of a large retail chain. By the end of the second week of its idea system pilot, the staff's ideas had permanently freed up the equivalent of two hours per employee every week. As the saying goes, "Never be too busy to find out how to be less busy."

In most situations, these early time-saving ideas combined with the scheduling discretion of managers are all that is needed to make the time available. However, sometimes one of the management systems blocks such moves, and the involvement of higher-level managers is required to fix the problem.

A number of years ago, a medical products division of a Fortune 500 company asked us to help improve its idea system. When we talked with front-line workers, the primary reason for the system's poor performance quickly emerged. The division's cost allocation system required that every minute of each front-line employee's time had to be charged to the production of a specific product. The simple fact that there was no job code for improvement time made it impossible for people to work on their ideas on company time. Employees who wanted to work on ideas had to do so on their own time. This company was going to have to change the way it accounted for the time of its front-line workers if it wanted to improve the performance of its idea system.

One way to assure that employees have the time they need to work on ideas is to directly incorporate this time into the overall work schedule. At the Swedish truck maker Scania's main engine plant outside Stockholm, for example, the assembly line is shut down for twenty-six minutes once a week for every area to hold its idea meeting. Furthermore, each team (typically nine to fourteen people) is deliberately overstaffed by two people in part to give team members enough time to implement improvement ideas. This resource commitment is a major reason that the company has been able to routinely improve overall productivity by 12 to 15 percent every year.

Aligning Funding for Ideas

Even small ideas often need a little money or a few supplies to implement. The key question here is, Can employees easily get the resources they need to develop and implement their ideas? Most organizations have never really dealt with large quantities of front-line ideas, so they are not set up to provide these resources in a streamlined manner. In some organizations, resources are so tightly controlled that front-line workers find it impossible to get what they need.

We encountered a poignant example of such tight control during the pilot stage of an idea system in the special orders department of a national retailer. A worker in that department did a lot of stapling as part of her job. She would often need to staple through cardboard to keep paperwork and samples together. Frequently, her attempts would go awry, and she would have to remove the mangled staples and start over. On days when she had a lot of such work to do, she would go home with very sore hands. Her solution: get an electric stapler. Her team and supervisor thought it was an excellent idea. But when she submitted the request to the supplies department, she was told that her job classification did not entitle her to an electric stapler. Undaunted, she stopped by a local Walmart on her way home that evening, purchased her own electric stapler, and brought it into work the next day. The new stapler dramatically increased her productivity and meant she no longer left work with sore hands. Everything was fine until she ran out of staples and requested some more. The response was that because she was not entitled to an electric stapler, she was not entitled to get any staples for it, either.

Restrictive and petty purchasing policies like this one make it hard for people to implement ideas. Even when specific purchases are technically allowed, sometimes the checks and balances incorporated into the purchasing process make it bureaucratic and frustrating for employees. We encountered one such situation while piloting an idea system at a medium-sized specialty manufacturer in New England. One of the first ideas to come in was from a machine operator who wanted to eliminate an irritating problem that cost him about fifteen minutes every day. At the end of each shift, he was required to shut off his machine and check its fluid levels and settings. Because he needed a light to see inside it, he would have to go to the tool room, check out a trouble light, return to his work area, plug in the light, string the wire over to his machine, open it up, check the necessary levels, and make any required adjustments. Then he would have to close the machine back up, unplug the light, recoil the wire, and take it back to the tool room to check it back in. His idea: purchase a flashlight with a magnetic back—for about $10—and stick it to the inside of his machine. It would then take only a minute for him to do all his checks. His team and supervisor liked the idea and approved it. But when we checked on the status of unimplemented ideas two months later, we found that the machine operator didn't have his flashlight yet. His request was still tied up in purchasing.

The slow purchasing process both deterred ideas and cost the company a tremendous amount in unrealized cost savings. In this case, assume that the machine and operator costs totaled $100 per hour. The $10 flashlight would have saved fifteen minutes, or $25 per day, and paid for itself the first time it was used! Instead, its arrival was delayed for more than fifty work days, potentially costing the company $1,250 in unrealized savings (50 days × $25 per day). Clearly, this company's purchasing process was poorly aligned for ideas.

These types of problems, and the frustration that accompanies them, can easily be addressed with modest budgets and streamlined purchasing processes for small front-line ideas. Some organizations give each team and its leader a small monthly idea budget—say, between $100 and $500—and allow them to make direct purchases with a company credit card or on account from specified vendors. Other companies allow teams or departments to spend a small amount on each idea, perhaps up to $100, using a stream-lined purchasing process. Although some managers are initially nervous about giving front-line teams and supervisors such spending authority, in our experience, the front-line teams and departments typically appreciate the trust shown in them, are very careful with the money, and the payback periods for their purchases are generally very short. And besides, middle and upper managers can—and should—review each team's purchasing records on a monthly basis. It is much easier and quicker to operate this way than to have to give separate permission for each small request.

Aligning Support Functions for Ideas

Before launching the pilot at the New England specialty manufacturer discussed earlier, the CEO had waved aside the concerns of his maintenance manager. He told the manager that for the duration of the three-month pilot, he was to make it a top priority to help workers in the pilot areas implement their ideas. At the end of the very successful pilot, the CEO polled his managers to see how many would support launching an idea system companywide. All of them were eager to do so, except the maintenance manager.

"I really can't support it," he said. "The pilot process alone nearly killed us. We had to postpone a lot of other maintenance work just to keep up with all the ideas."

Many ideas require the help of support functions such as information technology, maintenance, engineering, or purchasing. But these functions are typically not resourced, staffed, or tasked to support front-line ideas. If, in addition to their "normal" work, support functions are suddenly required to help implement large numbers of front-line ideas, they will be quickly overwhelmed, as that maintenance manager was.

Leaders of idea-driven organizations make sure their support functions are tasked and staffed to respond rapidly to front-line ideas. For example, when Allianz China's new chief information officer asked CEO Wilf Blackburn for permission to hire an additional IT technician, Blackburn's response was, "You can hire as many people as you need. But I never want to hear that an idea has not been implemented because of a backlog in IT." At Brasilata, the Brazilian company discussed in Chapter 1, special teams in each of its four manufacturing centers are dedicated *solely* to helping implement ideas. Each team consists of five or six members—including engineers, mechanics, an electrician, and a toolmaker. (More on Brasilata's system in the next chapter.)

Aligning support functions for front-line ideas can be challenging. It is never clear before an idea system is launched precisely *how much* of *what kind* of help will be needed from *which* support functions. Managers are understandably reluctant to commit additional resources before gaining some experience with ideas. This is why practically every high-performing idea system is launched with a shortage of support function resources in one area or another. To prevent their idea initiatives from stalling, managers must stand ready to react quickly as stress points emerge. Until the new levels of support resource needs become clearer, managers can temporarily add or reallocate resources, contract out for more support, ration support resources, or limit the number of ideas from each team that can call on specific support function resources.

Before launching his idea system, Brasilata's CEO did not sit down and calculate that his company would need eighteen more support people. Nor did Pete Wilson of Pyromation hire consultants to determine how much he would have to staff up his maintenance department in order to give his teams the support they needed to implement their ideas. What these two men did was to reallocate resources to where they were needed in a mea-sured fashion as the situation evolved.

ALIGNING POLICIES AND RULES

The word *policy* derives from the sixteenth-century French word *police*. In an organizational setting, policies are guiding principles or rules intended to police—that is, to direct, limit, and control—people's decisions and actions. Good policies streamline processes, save time, ensure fair treat-ment of employees, prevent fraud and ethical problems, assure high-levels of customer service, and make certain that money is spent wisely.

But most organizations have their share of bad policies as well. Such policies create unnecessary bureaucracy, raise the cost of performing tasks, annoy customers and employees, and generally impede progress. They can also directly or indirectly hinder the flow of ideas. A significant amount of the work in realigning an organization for ideas involves rooting out and then modifying or eliminating these idea-hampering policies. As with every element of the management system, keeping an organization's poli-cies aligned for ideas is an ongoing effort, as existing policies are changed and new ones are introduced all the time.

Even a single bad policy can cause an otherwise sound idea initiative to fail. Some years ago, the new CEO of a midsize utility company in the northeastern United States was under severe pressure from his board to cut costs. He spent the first several weeks visiting the company's front-line operations. During this process, he was struck by the number of good ideas he received from front-line employees. Not surprisingly, one of his early initiatives was to set up an idea system to systematically gather these ideas. His system was basically sound, but he made one crucial mistake: in his enthusiasm to generate quick results, he instituted a policy to ensure that the *estimated* cost savings from ideas would be immediately reflected in the company's bottom line. He ordered that as soon as an idea was implemented, its projected savings were to be pulled from the appropri-ate middle manager's budget.

This policy devastated the idea initiative. Middle managers told us pri-vately that, because the savings projected by the suggestion system office were always optimistic (the office was evaluated on the system's savings, after all), it was dangerous for them to implement ideas. The controller would immediately take more from their budgets than the idea would actually save. So the only way for middle managers to protect their budgets was to quietly sit on approved ideas. At one point while we were studying this company, an eighteen-month backlog of unimplemented ideas was costing the company an estimated $2 million per year in unrealized savings. More important, as employees saw their ideas going unused, the stream of new ideas slowed to a trickle.

Most policies have unintended consequences, many of which the policymakers never become aware of. As far as we know, that utility company CEO never realized how his policy undermined his own goals and how his middle managers were being forced to use their creativity to come up with delaying tactics for ideas rather than ways to implement them more quickly.

Policymaking is not the exclusive domain of senior management. In fact, a complicating issue with policies is that they are typically made by many people at different levels working in different parts of the organization, each of whom is trying to deal with problems from his or her perspective. For example, IT dictates how it will prioritize requests for help in order to optimize the use of its staff; or purchasing sets policies requiring multiple bids in an effort to ensure the company doesn't overspend for goods and services. The resulting tangled web of policies can create significant obstacles for the rapid implementation of ideas.

In many situations, bad policies can be dealt with informally or even through the idea system. But in complex environments, a separate system may be needed to thoroughly check into the reasons the policies were put in place and to determine all the ramifications of changing them. A good example of such a system was the "Kill Stupid Rules" (KSR) program set up at a large U.S. bank. Its purpose was to empower front-line bank employees to point out policies and rules that, from their perspectives, degraded customer service unnecessarily.

The name "Kill Stupid Rules" was memorable, as well as a clever way to admit that managers occasionally created stupid policies and to invite employees to point them out. As the director of the KSR system put it, the bank needed to know whether a policy to solve one problem had inadvertently created other problems. Before we describe the KSR process and the lessons to be learned from it, let's look at some examples of policies that were successfully killed.

- Whenever business customers deposited large quantities of coins, they were charged a small processing fee. But as one employee pointed out, when *non*customers exchanged large amounts of coins for banknotes, they were not charged this fee. In other words, if you wanted the bank to count your coins, you were better off *not* being a customer. The reason for this policy, it turned out, was that the bank's computer system was not set up to charge noncustomers. After weighing the revenue from coin counting against the negative impact on customer service, the bank dropped the fee.

- The process to remove a deceased spouse from a couple's joint account required that the account be closed and a new one opened for the survivor. An employee pointed out that this was time-consuming, insensitive to the grieving spouse, and practically invited that person to take her or his business elsewhere. It turned out that the policy had been created years earlier by the legal department in an overkill response to federal regulations enacted to protect the estates of deceased individuals. After some research by KSR analysts, it became clear that a valid death certificate was sufficient evidence to simply remove a deceased partner from an account.

- When adding a signer to a business account, businesses had to resubmit a new signature form with *all* signers. Bank staff would then have to reinput all the data by hand and rescan each signature. With some accounts having forty or more signers, this was a huge waste of time for both customers and the bank. The only justification that could be found for the policy was that no one was sure if the system could properly retain the information on existing signers when a new one was added. After assurance from the IT department that no existing signatures would be lost, the policy was killed.

Here is how KSR worked. An employee would submit a KSR request via a call or e-mail to the KSR team. The proposed policy change went to one of several full-time KSR analysts for initial review. The analyst first called the submitter to get more information about the policy in question—which also showed the suggester that the proposed policy change was being followed up on. If the analyst agreed that the policy should be reviewed, the next step was an initial analysis to find out why the policy existed, who it impacted and in what way, and what it would take to change it. Each area of the bank had an assigned contact person that the KSR analyst dealt with. Experience had shown that the more thoroughly the initial case was researched, the easier the rest of the process went.

Once the preparatory research was done, the proposed change was taken to the monthly "User Group" meeting. The group, consisting of some twenty people from the bank's key functional areas (e.g., compliance, audit, legal, operations, product, staff support, and training), typically discussed up to twenty-five proposed policy changes in each meeting. The analysts explained the issues involved with each policy and proposed some initial options for changing it. The group decided whether the policy change was worth pursuing further, determined whose input was needed, and identified any specific areas of concern. The analyst then did any additional research required and managed the final policy change process.

The bank gave us copies of several analyst research logs in which every contact made and each piece of information obtained was recorded. The logs demonstrate the extensive research, attention to detail, and amount of communication needed to change a policy in a complex and highly interconnected organization. Some of the policies have more than a hundred entries, such as "Talk to X," "Sent e-mail to Y asking for clarification," "We have 60,000 accounts to which this policy applies," "Got e-mail from Z—she is OK with the change," "Get new verbiage for marketing documents," and "Conducted survey of 120 employees—32% report customer complaints on this topic." Over the lifetime of the KSR process, it killed or amended hundreds of bad policies and empowered the bank's front-line employees to remove policy-related problems and impediments much more easily than their peers at other institutions. (Unfortunately, the KSR program was killed when the bank was acquired by an even larger bank, one not known for its enlightened management or customer service.)

The KSR process was more involved than a normal idea process, because it is difficult to anticipate all the ramifications of removing or changing a policy. What may seem like an obviously bad policy is sometimes in place for very good reasons.

An important lesson that the bank drew from its KSR experience was that in order to reduce the painful process of changing policies, managers need to be more thoughtful and skillful when making policies; and when creating new policies, they need to document the reasons for them.

A Brief Primer on Policymaking

Given the extensive use of policies in organizations, it is surprising how little training managers typically get in policymaking. Equipping managers with some basic knowledge in this area, together with an appreciation of how policies directly and indirectly affect the flow of ideas, will dramatically improve the effectiveness of the policies they make.

Most policies are created to prevent problems—real or perceived. While the new policies may solve the policymakers' immediate problems, they frequently create more and bigger problems elsewhere.

Take, for example, what happened to the new director of R&D at a high-technology Fortune 500 company. During his first week, the director noticed that many of his scientists and engineers were not at their desks by the official 8 a.m. starting time and were gone before the 5 p.m. official closing time. Determined that there would be no slacking off on his watch, he issued a new policy: everyone was required to be at their desks by 8 a.m. and was not to leave before 5 p.m. The director began walking around to check which workers were at their work stations, and which were not.

The scientists and engineers, most of whom were accomplished professionals with advanced degrees, resented such a demeaning directive. It showed how little the director understood about the nature of their work and that he did not appreciate that they were intrinsically motivated people who typically worked fifty hours or more per week, often taking work home with them. In fact, many started work well *before* 8 a.m., and 7 a.m.

breakfast meetings were common. By the time the director arrived closer to 8 a.m., many of his scientists were already working in other areas of the company, and many didn't get back to their desks until long after the director had left for the day. Besides, what was wrong with leaving work early to watch your daughter's soccer game after putting in sixty hours the week before to meet a deadline?

The employees responded collectively by *following* the new director's policy to the letter. Each researcher began arriving at his desk *precisely* at 8 and leaving *immediately* at 5. Soon, the lab started missing critical milestones and deadlines—something that rarely happened under the previous leadership—and new product ideas all but dried up. It took the director months to figure out why.

Most of the company's truly novel and most profitable products could be traced to ideas that were unrelated to the researchers' official work assignments. In the past, the researchers would come in early or stay late to work on such ideas. They would test their concepts or meet with colleagues to discuss and develop the ideas further. Only when an idea seemed to hold promise did they bring it to management, which could then launch it as an official project.

This new lab director made the same mistake that many managers do when creating a policy: he focused too narrowly on a specific perceived problem. He neither verified his assumptions nor thought about the broader context and the tangible and intangible implications of his policy. Consequently, he created new problems that were much more damaging.

A useful framework for policymaking is the Policy Analysis Matrix in Table 4.1. The R&D director focused on eliminating a problem (Quadrant 1) without considering the other three quadrants. To begin with, he did not consider the cost of his new policy in terms of the advantages it would eliminate (Quadrant 2). The policy demotivated an already hardworking workforce. With the new policy, he (unwittingly) accepted an 8-to-5 workforce that would be less innovative and was willing to miss important deadlines (Quadrant 3). As far as we could tell, the policy retained or created no advantages for him (Quadrant 4), other than his feeling of being in control and that his people were not slacking off.

TABLE 4.1 The Policy Analysis Matrix

	Problems	Advantages
Eliminate	**Quadrant 1** Problems the policy will eliminate	**Quadrant 2** Advantages the policy will eliminate
Retain/Create	**Quadrant 3** Problems the policy will retain/create	**Quadrant 4** Advantages the policy will retain/create

Had he gathered more data and thoughtfully considered this aspect of the issue, he would more likely have chosen to accept a few people occasionally coming in late or leaving early in order to retain his workforce's productivity and high level of intrinsic motivation.

There are usually more effective ways to govern people's actions than to issue sweeping edicts, which can easily create a host of additional problems. If the director was concerned about his people slacking off, a more nuanced and targeted approach would have worked much better. Had he discussed his concerns with his managers, he would have learned that the problem was not nearly as pervasive as it first appeared, and that they could deal with the few actual transgressors individually. This would have been a much better solution than dropping a policy bomb that turned the majority of his scientists into collateral damage.

There is a natural tendency to reach for policies when trying to eliminate problems. They appear to offer quick and easy solutions. But policies are generally blunt instruments with a limited ability to take situational nuances into account. They may work well in some circumstances, but in most situations a more subtle, flexible, or targeted approach will be more effective at addressing the underlying problem.

When a policy *is* the best tool for the job, it should not be created without thoughtful analysis and great care to identify as many of its ramifications as possible. The Policy Analysis Matrix can help the decision maker more broadly frame potential policy solutions with a better understanding of their consequences.

So far, we have discussed only how to avoid the negative side effects of policies. But we should also note that well-considered policies can be very beneficial, sometimes even *because* they are blunt instruments and leave little room for any nuance or interpretation. We have come across a number of organizations with policies incorporated into their idea systems that energize and stimulate idea efforts, and articulate clear commitments about how ideas will be managed. Here are some of the more memorable examples we have seen:

- When Roger Milliken, former CEO of Milliken Corporation, the global textile company, started his company's idea system, he established two important policies. First, every idea would be acknowledged within twenty-four hours and acted on within seventy-two (i.e., it would be rejected, implementation of it would begin, or further study of it would be initiated). Second, improvement ideas were always to be put *first* on the agenda at every management meeting.
- As discussed earlier, many organizations have policies that give front-line teams specified spending authorities to implement ideas. The highest spending authority we have seen was in the early 2000s at a Dana facility in Missouri (Dana is a Tier 1 automobile industry supplier) which gave its front-line teams up to $500 to spend, without management approval, to implement each idea. Team members told us that when tackling bigger problems, they would often fund their efforts by attacking the problems with a series of smaller ideas, which allowed them to gin up a bigger budget.
- At the Swedish ventilation company Fresh, any spending from the team's idea budget must be voted on by the team itself. The team's manager alone does not have the authority to make spending decisions related to this budget.
- ThedaCare, the health care provider discussed in Chapter 2, has a policy that 8 a.m. to 10 a.m. is a "meeting-free zone," so managers can do their *gemba* walks and support improvement efforts.

ALIGNING PROCESSES
AND PROCEDURES

Some years ago, the vice president of quality at a medium-size software firm called one of us to ask for help in getting his company ISO 9001 certified (ISO 9001 is the International Standards Organization's standard for an organization's quality management system). During our initial conversation, the vice president explained his problem.

"We [the quality department] have already written all of the procedures, but we can't get our employees to follow them. We need your team to make that happen."

The vice president's request dropped us right into the thick of a long-standing debate over the question of whether it is better for management to impose standardized procedures from above, or to have them developed and owned by the people doing the work. This question was a central point of debate in the early days of scientific management between the movement's two most eminent champions and their followers. Frederick Taylor believed that management should write the procedures based on its own analysis of the work, and then impose them on the workers as a means of control. Frank Gilbreth also sought to use best practices, but he realized that a great deal of knowledge about how best to do the work resided with those who actually did it. In his view, the procedures were the basis for continuous improvement, which should be driven by the people doing the work, with one important proviso:

> *It is seldom appreciated by the layman that the only inventions and improvements that are not wanted are those that are offered by the employee before he has first qualified on the standard method of procedure. . . . The condition precedent to an audience for offering a suggestion for improvement is to have proved that the suggester knows the standard method, and can do the work in the standard way of standard quality in the standard time. Having thus qualified, he is in a position to know whether or not his new suggestion is a real improvement.*[1]

By trying to force his procedures on the workforce, that VP had lost the benefits of having his front-line workers develop them, and then continue to think about how to improve them. What he should have done, and what we advised him to do, was to ask his front people to document how they actually did their work. Only *then* should the VP have had his staff review the worker-generated draft procedures to see if they complied with the requirements of the ISO 9001 standard. Where they did not, his staff should have provided coaching and worked with the front-line workers to figure out how best to modify their work methods to meet the standards.

This more inclusive approach might have taken a little extra time up front, but it would also have gotten the company certified much more quickly. It would have eliminated the need for management to force front-line workers into following management-designed procedures, only to discover after much pain that many of them were impractical and needed to be changed. When, from the start, the documented procedures accurately reflect how the work is performed, the foundation is laid for ongoing process improvement.

Ideally, processes and procedures should reflect the organization's accumulated knowledge at any given point in time, and they should be constantly modified and tweaked as new knowledge emerges. One of the fundamental differences between traditional and idea-driven organizations lies in who owns the processes—that is, who is responsible for their performance and who has the authority to change them. It is impossible to have a high-performing idea system without the processes and procedures being owned by the people using them. Many of their ideas will be for improvements to the very processes and procedures they work with; and the quicker they can implement these ideas, the faster the organization will capture the new knowledge in them, and the faster the organization will improve. If management owns the procedures, the rate of improvement is limited by the amount of time that *management* can commit to improving them and its incomplete understanding of what goes on at the front-line level.

Unfortunately, shifting ownership of processes and procedures to the front lines is more than a matter of simply deciding to trust employees and then dumping the responsibility on them. It requires careful goal alignment, well-defined responsibilities and authorities, systematic accountability, and systems to assure that front-line people have the proper skills and information. To us, the common lack of consideration for these elements explains why so many organizational empowerment initiatives experience false starts and failures.

ALIGNING EVALUATION AND REWARD SYSTEMS

Evaluation and reward schemes are notoriously difficult to get right. So before trying to integrate ideas into existing schemes, it is important to understand what actually motivates people to step forward with ideas.

An exercise we often use in our seminars sheds light on this question. We ask participants to do the following:

1. Think of an idea that you came up with at work and brought to the attention of your colleagues or boss.
2. Write down what caused you to have this idea and what made you step forward with it.
3. Together with the other people at your table, share and discuss your answers.

Typical responses include "It made my job easier," "It saved me time," "It eliminated a problem or source of frustration," "It improved customer service," "I wanted to help the company," and "I felt pride about my work"—all of which are expressions of *intrinsic* motivation. Rarely does anyone say, "I did it for a reward." This exercise illustrates that people naturally want to share ideas and do not need to be bribed to do so. In fact, we recommend that organizations not set up a separate system of rewards for individual ideas, as many suggestion box–type systems used to do, as this approach creates serious behavioral issues and misalignments on many levels. (For more on the dysfunction created by rewards for individual ideas, see Chapter 3 of *Ideas Are Free*.)

Ideas should be treated just like any other important aspect of performance. Every organization has mechanisms to evaluate and reward its people; these include performance reviews, bonuses, merit increases, and promotions. In idea-driven organizations, where ideas are a normal part of everyone's job, idea performance needs to be integrated into these mechanisms, too.

In our experience, it is usually relatively straightforward to do this. Most personnel evaluation schemes already include competencies such as "Willingness to change," "Creativity," "Adaptability," and "Improvement orientation" that can be easily adapted to include idea performance. And many idea-driven organizations have linked bonuses to idea performance as well.

CONCLUSION

Three elements remain to be covered in the Framework for Alignment (Figure 3.1). Chapter 7 addresses the "skills" element, which is best explained after the idea management processes have been laid out in Chapters 5 and 6. And because of the integrated nature of "culture" and "behavior," they are discussed throughout the book.

Realignment for ideas is a game-changer. Without this piece, it is impossible for an organization to become truly idea driven. People cannot be expected to offer their ideas if every day the way the organization is structured, managed and led tells them these ideas are not welcome. And once an organization is aligned, keeping it aligned requires constant vigilance and ongoing effort.

With this in mind, we are now ready to turn to the "how-to" of setting up, launching, and managing the idea process itself.

KEY POINTS

✓ An organization's management systems are generally set up and evolve incrementally over time with little thought given to their impact on the flow of ideas. Consequently, the management systems in most organizations are seriously misaligned for bottom-up ideas.

✓ Ideas are an investment in the future. Leaders have to give their employees time to work on ideas, together with small budgets and easy access to assistance from support functions, if they expect their organizations to improve and innovate at a rapid rate.

✓ Policies that directly or indirectly reduce the flow of ideas need to be modified or eliminated. This process can be very challenging. Policies are typically made by many people in different parts of the organization, each of whom is dealing with problems from his or her perspective, with little thought to how these policies may affect the flow of ideas.

✓ Given the extensive use of policies in organizations, it is surprising how little training managers typically get in policymaking. Equipping managers with some basic knowledge in this area will dramatically improve the effectiveness of the policies they make.

✓ It is impossible to be an idea-driven organization without the processes and procedures being owned by the people using them. Processes and procedures should reflect the organization's accumulated knowledge at any given point in time and should be constantly modified and tweaked as new knowledge emerges.

✓ Ideas should be treated just like any other important aspect of performance and integrated into an organization's existing performance reviews, bonuses, merit increases, and promotions. This is usually quite straightforward to do.

5

How Effective Idea Processes Work

IN 1992, MARTIN EDELSTON, CEO of Boardroom Inc., a Connecticut-based publisher, hired the iconic management guru Peter Drucker to come and spend a day at his company. Edelston had no particular goals in mind for the visit; he simply wanted Drucker to take a look at his company and tell him how to improve it. At the end of the day, Drucker gave him a piece of advice that would transform the company: ask every employee to come to his or her weekly departmental meeting with an idea to improve the company or his or her own work. Edelston took the advice and started right in.

Initially, wanting to maintain control, he personally reviewed and approved every idea. His method was to go through the week's ideas on weekends while working out on his exercise bike. He joked with us that this took him so much time that he became extremely fit.

One Sunday, however, as he was working through a stack of suggestions, Edelston encountered one for a software improvement from a programmer in the IT department. Because he didn't understand the idea, on Monday morning, he hunted down the programmer and asked him to explain it. Half an hour later, Edelston walked away still confused.

Then came an epiphany. Edelston had hired the programmer for his expertise. He understood far more about the company's IT systems than Edelston ever would. Why should Edelston be the one to decide whether the software change made sense or not? And, in general, weren't decisions about ideas best made by those most familiar with the situation involved? Realizing that he was only getting in the way, Edelston changed the rules. Effective immediately, most decisions about ideas would be made by the front-line employees in their weekly department meetings. The only ideas he needed to see were the ones involving significant investments or multiple departments. Making all other decisions at the lowest possible level in the company would result in less work, better decisions, and faster implementation. (See *Ideas Are Free* for more on the Boardroom story.)

But if Edelston personally had to review and evaluate every idea, he was merely running a *suggestion* system, and the success of the system would be limited by his knowledge and time. The underlying assumption in a suggestion system—whether the suggestions are collected in a box or online—is that management knows best. Regular employees cannot be trusted to do what is best for the organization, because either they lack the necessary knowledge and judgment, or they will put their personal interests ahead of those of the organization. So the "adults" have to be involved in approving even the smallest changes. Under such a regime, it is hardly surprising that management becomes a bottleneck and employees feel disempowered. This is one reason that most suggestion systems get less than half an idea per person per year and implement less than a third of those.

Edelston's epiphany was precisely what he needed to create a high-performing idea system. The quantity and quality of ideas soared, and by the mid-1990s the company was averaging over a hundred ideas per employee per year, with implementation rates over 90 percent.

When leaders feel they can trust their workers to make decisions about their own ideas, the question becomes how to design a system that operationalizes this trust. In the rest of this chapter, we describe the three archetypes of high-performing idea processes that do just that: the *kaizen teian,* idea meeting, and idea board processes.

THE *KAIZEN TEIAN* PROCESS

We first encountered the *kaizen teian* (Japanese for "improvement suggestion") process—which we consider the first generation of high-performing idea systems—in Japan in the mid-1980s, where it was being used in many large companies. By the early 1990s, as leading Japanese companies began to globalize their manufacturing, they introduced this process to the rest of the world. Although the *kaizen teian* system historically grew out of the suggestion box process, and the two processes have many outward similarities, the *kaizen teian* approach evolved to mitigate or eliminate most of the flaws of the suggestion box. The best way to understand how this archetype works is to look at an example. We have chosen to describe the system of Brasilata, the Brazilian can maker we discussed in Chapter 1, to demonstrate that *kaizen teian* can also work in a non-Japanese setting.

CEO Antonio Texeira started the company's idea system in the early 1990s, after reading a number of Japanese books and articles, and becoming intrigued by the dramatic results produced by *kaizen teian* processes. Today, Brasilata gets around 150 ideas per person each year, implements 90 percent of them, and is ranked as one of the most innovative companies in Brazil.

Each of Brasilata's four facilities around Brazil has a full-time staff to support the idea system. At the company's main operation in São Paolo, for example, ideas are processed by a team of seven experienced workers on temporary assignments from the factory floor (whose knowledge allows them to understand the ideas better and gives them credibility with suggesters). In addition, a team of two mechanics, two engineers, a toolmaker, and an electrician is dedicated to helping implement the ideas. Similar teams exist in the company's other three facilities.

There are two ways to submit ideas, online or on paper. To facilitate online access, Brasilata set up a number of Internet cafés throughout its facilities, but some employees still find it easier to write their ideas on paper. The paper ideas are put into special collection boxes, from which they are picked up twice a day and entered into the system within twenty-four hours.

Whenever possible, employees implement their own ideas *before* submitting them. They simply approach their coordinators (Brasilata's term for front-line managers) who can approve ideas that cost less than 100 reais (about $50) to implement. A director (the coordinator's boss) can authorize up to 5,000 reais (some $2,500); above that amount, ideas go directly to the CEO. About 70 percent of ideas are implemented directly by the workers themselves, and a further 10 percent by the coordinators. The remaining 20 percent are escalated or become the responsibility of one of the implementation teams.

When an employee does not have the authority or ability to implement an idea him- or herself, that worker is expected to recommend the best person to review it. Often, this person is the employee's coordinator, although it could be anyone in the company. Whoever ends up getting the idea has seven days to evaluate and respond to it before the item turns red on that person's idea summary screen. Once an idea is approved, it must be implemented within 45 days. Once a month, the CEO reviews a list of ideas that have gone red or whose implementation is overdue, and follows up with delinquent managers with what a group of coordinators told us is often a "very hard talk."

All in all, out of almost a thousand employees in the company, more than forty work full-time on processing or implementing employee ideas. Additional support is provided by Brasilata's technical support departments. Coordinators told us that they spend about 10 percent of their time working with employee ideas.

Kaizen teian–type systems are rare in organizations without some kind of connection to Japan. As stated earlier, they are essentially traditional suggestion box–type systems that have been highly streamlined to mitigate their inherent limitations. To work well, they also require a culture of improvement that strongly encourages individuals to step forward with ideas. Because they depend on a strong culture, building high-performing *kaizen teian* systems requires persistence and discipline over a period of many years. It took several decades for Brasilata to get its system up to its current level of performance. We believe that the extraordinary patience and sustained discipline needed to build and nurture the unusually strong improvement culture that drives a *kaizen teian* system explains why so few organizations use this type of system today.

TEAM-BASED PROCESSES

Most organizations setting up high-performing idea systems today use the second and third archetypes of idea processes, the idea meeting and idea board processes, which are both team based. They can be ramped up much more quickly than *kaizen teian* systems, as they are integrated into the way that regular work is done, so they can start producing good results in a relatively short period of time. Team-based processes are designed so that people bring "opportunities for improvement" (OFIs) to their work groups or departments. An OFI is a problem, an opportunity, or an idea. (As an opportunity is the flip side of a problem, from now on we will use the word *problem* to mean both problems and opportunities.)

It is important that both processes encourage people to offer problems as well as ideas. Most people have learned through experience to view problems as negative, to be avoided or hidden. After all, no one wants to be blamed for them or to be viewed as a complainer for bringing them up. But because every idea begins with a problem, teams must learn to *seek out and embrace problems*, instead of avoiding them.

Opening the process up to problems will significantly increase both the quantity and quality of a team's ideas. The quantity of ideas goes up because often the person who identifies a problem has no idea about how to solve it, but a teammate does. The quality of ideas is improved because the team brings multiple perspectives and much more knowledge to bear on the problem, so the solution will be better thought out. Sometimes, an idea is an unworkable solution to a real problem. In rejecting the idea, it is easy for people to miss the underlying problem. But by returning to it, the team can often find an effective solution.

We came across a good example of how this works at Springfield Technical Community College (STCC), a college serving more than nine thousand students in the inner city of Springfield, Massachusetts. STCC is one of the few institutions of higher education we are aware of with a high-performing idea system. A number of years ago, when the system was launched, during the first idea meeting of a team in one of the pilot areas, an employee posted an idea: "Let's put posters and table tents around campus to remind students to use the online campus system that allows them to check grades, pay bills, preregister for classes, etc." STCC's idea board process gave every team member two votes on which ideas the department should work on, and no one voted for her idea. Struck by this, toward the end of the session, the facilitator asked the suggester to explain the underlying problem.

The problem, she explained, was that students were not using the campus online system and instead were stopping into departmental and student support service offices to ask staff for the information they wanted. "Every semester, employees spend countless hours helping students who could easily be helping themselves," she told the group. Hence her idea: advertise the online campus system to get students to use it.

The team agreed that students were not using the online tool and that they could easily answer their own questions if they did. "Why, then," the facilitator asked, "did no one vote for this idea?"

The answer turned out to be that the idea had already been tried in several different forms and had failed. Many departments had created posters, signs, and table tent cards to advertise the online system, but the advertising had made little difference. Students continued to ask staff for the information they wanted.

The facilitator realized that, in rejecting the proposed solution, the team had also lost the opportunity to work on solving the underlying problem. But when she brought the group back to the problem, its members realized that just because advertising had failed, it didn't mean that they couldn't solve the problem another way. After a brief discussion, the group agreed that if students knew how to use the online system, they would. In other words, the root cause of the problem was a lack of training, not a lack of awareness. So the team proposed that the college implement self-help stations at various campus registration sites staffed by work-study students whose jobs would be to assist their peers in understanding and fully utilizing the online campus system. The idea proved successful, and the college estimated that it saved the staff almost seven hundred hours per year.

Most teams start out by wanting to work only with ideas and viewing their task as simply giving the thumbs-up or thumbs-down to each. It takes time and effort for teams to learn how to move smoothly back and forth between problems and potential solutions as the situation dictates, but when they do, they will produce significantly more and better ideas.

The Idea Meeting Process

We first encountered idea meetings at Boardroom in 1996. At the time, as we mentioned earlier, the company's weekly meetings were generating more than a hundred ideas per employee every year, with implementation rates over 90 percent.

In the generic idea meeting process, people bring their OFIs to a regularly scheduled meeting. This could be a dedicated idea meeting or a standing agenda item in a regular team/department meeting. The meeting is usually held every week or two. Any less frequent than this makes it difficult for the idea process to gain traction and become a regular part of everyone's work routine.

The facilitator begins the meeting by reviewing the progress made on actions assigned at the previous meeting and addressing any issues that have arisen with them, and then calls on each member to read out and explain his or her OFIs. Each OFI is then discussed and the group decides what actions (if any) it wants to take on it. These actions could be to conduct further research into the issue, to implement an agreed-on idea, to escalate an idea to the next level of management, or to put it in a "parking lot" to revisit it sometime in the future.

Actions requiring follow-up work are assigned to individual team members and then entered into a tracking system, which is often a simple spreadsheet. This tracking sheet includes all pertinent information about the OFIs: what actions are to be taken, who is responsible for taking them, and the anticipated completion dates. It also records ideas that have been escalated and OFIs that the team wishes to table for possible action later.

The Idea Board Process

The idea board approach is essentially an idea meeting process in which each team or department manages its ideas using an idea board. This board might be a whiteboard, any other type of visible board, or an electronic flat-screen, placed prominently in the team's workplace. For simplicity here, we will explain the process using a whiteboard.

The specific design of the boards varies greatly across organizations, but at a minimum all of them allow team members to post OFIs, record action items, and track their progress. Figure 5.1 illustrates a basic idea board layout for a team or department. The boxes across the top half are used to collect the team's OFIs for each of its designated focus areas, which should correspond to the goals that have been rolled down from above. The bottom half of the board is used to manage the actions being taken. We will explain the design of this idea board in more detail shortly.

The idea board process has several advantages over the idea meeting approach. The boards' highly visual nature reminds people about the

FIGURE 5.1 Sample team idea board

Accounts Payable

Focus Area #1	Focus Area #2	Focus Area #3	
Ideas for Implementation		**Implementer**	**Due Date**

importance of ideas, keeps them focused on key team goals, and creates social pressure to complete assigned tasks on time. It also allows higher-level managers to see instantly how active each idea group is and to review its current improvement projects.

The Process. A typical weekly idea meeting begins with a review of the status of previously assigned actions. Completed actions, including ideas that the team has worked on and wishes to escalate, are recorded in a database and removed from the board, and the status of any actions that are still in progress is updated. Unanticipated delays on assigned OFIs are discussed and, if necessary, addressed with additional assignments.

Then the group turns to the OFIs posted on the top half of the board and prioritizes which ones to work on. Some of these will have been newly posted during the previous week; others will be holdovers that the group has not yet chosen to work on. The team decides what actions will be taken to move each of the chosen OFIs forward, assigns these actions with expected completion dates to team members, and records them on the bottom section of the board to manage follow-through.

The Board. As mentioned earlier, although all idea boards work in essentially the same way, their specific layout can vary considerably. On the basic board shown in Figure 5.1, the top is divided into three boxes, one for each of the team's goals or focus areas. (Recall that in Chapter 3, we discussed how idea-driven organizations carefully align each team's goals with the organization's overall strategic goals.) Team members post their individual OFIs in the box they pertain to. Some board designs have more than three focus areas or include additional boxes for other purposes, such as one-time themes, "parking lots" for ideas put on hold, escalated ideas, or OFIs that don't fit any of the focus areas.

Depending on the circumstances and nature of the department or team, the goals can be highly specific or relatively broad. For example, the focus areas picked by the warehouse manager at that Spanish/Portuguese electronics retailer described in Chapter 3 were "Shipments per week per employee," "Percentage of orders shipped same day and correctly," and "Inventory turnover." This level of specificity was very effective for the

well-defined task of filling orders in a distribution warehouse. In a less structured and more complex environment, more general focus areas might work
better. In the claims department of a U.K. insurance company, the focus
areas chosen were "productivity/efficiency," "customer service," and "reduction of rework." Management felt that more narrowly defined metrics such
as "claims processed per hour," "customer complaints" and "errors per 100
claims" would have been too restrictive and would have limited ideas.

From time to time, we are asked how OFIs should be posted on the
board. Some organizations use sticky notes, preprinted cards, or slips of
paper. Others ask employees to write on the board directly. Each approach
has advantages and disadvantages. Often, when people think of an OFI,
it is inconvenient to get to the board immediately. So if the OFI has to be
written on the board, it might be lost. If the system uses cards, a person can
carry them in a pocket or briefcase and write down OFIs as they come up
(even while at home or traveling) and post them on the board later. Posted
cards can also be easily moved, and OFIs on related topics can be clustered
easily without erasing and rewriting. Preprinted cards typically include
spaces for the submitter's name, the date, a description of the underlying
problem, and an idea to address it, if there is one. The name and date help
with accountability, and the explicit problem statement helps in getting the
group to consider the underlying problems and alternative solutions for
them. The advantage of writing directly on the board is that the OFIs are
more visible, and during the meeting people can see all the ideas at once.
This makes the idea meetings go faster and helps keep people engaged.

Teams are often concerned about publicly posting their problems on
boards that can be read by visitors or people from other departments. But
unless there is proprietary or sensitive information involved, making the
boards visible demonstrates that the team, and the entire organization, is
open to recognizing and addressing problems. In our experience, instead
of embarrassing the team in front of visitors, it invariably impresses them.

For example, the CEO of a medium-sized New England company once
hosted a group of bankers who were considering his company's application
for a major expansion loan. At one point, the bankers stopped in front of
an idea board and one of them asked what it was. The CEO explained that
the board showed some of that area's problems and what the employees

were doing about them. It also had some "before" and "after" photographs of completed projects. Later, the CEO told us that the moment those bankers realized the implications of what they saw on the board was also the moment when they decided to grant the loan. Companies that are open about their problems, and ensure that their people are constantly working to solve them, are the ones worth banking on—literally!

Publicly visible idea boards also communicate the specific issues a team is working on to employees and managers from other departments. People will often read *other* teams' boards out of curiosity and to get insights and ideas for their own teams. We are often asked whether people should be allowed to post OFIs on other teams' boards. In principle, this is something to encourage, but it can be a very sensitive area, as OFIs coming from outside the team can be viewed as criticisms. Our recommendation, at least until an organization's idea system and culture are mature, is that if someone has an OFI to share with another team, that person should recruit one of that team's members as a cosponsor.

Some organizations use dedicated electronic flat-screens as idea boards. One advantage of electronic boards is that they can easily be set up to allow team members to access them remotely at any time from their computers or mobile devices. In some situations, such as when team members are geographically dispersed, organizations take their boards and meetings completely online, typically using some kind of web-based project management application. While this reduces the quality of the team interactions somewhat, it does allow idea meetings to take place when face-to-face ones would be impossible.

FACILITATION

Because so much depends on drawing out the knowledge and creativity of team members, idea meetings must be well facilitated. Usually, facilitators are team leaders or supervisors, but they can also be members of the team. They do not have to be the most knowledgeable person in the room but must be skilled at managing a group process. Facilitators have to elicit input from all team members, particularly those who tend to be quiet. They must keep the group focused on issues that are largely within its domains and get it to prioritize the OFIs it wants to work on. They have to decide which OFIs the group should deal with quickly, which require more in-depth discussion, and which need more research. Facilitators have to get agreement on what actions to take, who will take them, and when they should be completed. And while keeping all this moving along briskly, they need to keep everybody engaged. Great facilitators even make meetings fun. Expert facilitation is critical to running effective idea meetings, and investing in training and coaching in this area pays quick dividends.

We have several tips on idea meeting facilitation. The first deals with larger ideas. Often a team will want to take on an idea that is too big to be completed in a week or two. Rather than assigning the entire task to a single person or small group, it is usually better to turn the idea into a project and break it down into smaller tasks. This allows the team to spread the tasks across many people and match their skills with the required work. The idea meetings then double as project meetings to monitor progress, assign new tasks, and decide on any adjustments needed as the project progresses.

A similar tactic can be used to incrementally attack large complex problems that are not resolvable with a single idea. By tackling such a problem with many small and easily implemented ideas, the team can incrementally reduce its negative impact and perhaps even completely solve it over time.

Second, ideas will often emerge that cannot be used immediately. Such ideas might include improvements requiring capital expenditures that need to wait for the next budget cycle, facility improvements that are best included in an upcoming renovation, modifications to software or equipment that are currently impractical but could be incorporated into the next upgrade, and product or service features that could be incorporated into future design changes. Such ideas should be recorded in one or more idea parking lots to be easily retrieved when the time is right.

Third, someone other than the facilitator should act as scribe in the meetings to record OFIs and decisions. A facilitator also serving as a scribe is distracted from the primary role of guiding the team as it addresses problems and develops ideas.

Fourth, facilitators need to know how to deal with ideas that cannot be implemented. Few things will shut down ideas faster than employees feeling their thoughts and ideas are not taken seriously. Otherwise good ideas might not be implementable for many possible reasons: money is not available; the ideas don't support the company's goals; other planned changes will supersede them; legal or regulatory restrictions may prohibit them. A good facilitator makes sure that the reasons for not going forward with an idea are drawn out and understood.

At this point, the facilitator has two choices: drop the idea, or, if appropriate, take the group back to the original problem to see whether it can take advantage of any underlying opportunities embedded in it.

Take, for example, what happened with one group we worked with. The director of a university alumni relations department had invited us to give a brief talk to her department on the benefits of starting an idea system, which we did. Several months later, she called us again. She told us that her department had enthusiastically set up a system and forged ahead. However, she and the staff had some concerns about how the process was working and wondered if we could come back and give them some additional help.

A few weeks later we went back and found the entire department of about thirty people assembled in a conference room. "Our biggest challenge," the director said to nods of agreement from around the room, "is that we have no difficulty thinking of good ideas, but we don't seem to have the time or resources to implement any of them."

We asked her for an example. She picked up the list of ideas that had come in so far and read out the first one: "Give everyone training in Excel.

"This is an excellent idea," she continued. "We all use Excel all the time. But when we looked into the cost of sending everyone to training, it was more than $15,000, and we would have had to shut down the office for two days."

"Who came up with this idea?" we asked, looking for the problem that triggered the idea. A woman in the back raised her hand.

"What made you think of it?" we asked her.

"I needed to make a [particular kind of] chart in Excel but couldn't figure out how to make it work," she told the group. "It made me think that we could all use some Excel training."

"I know how to make that kind of chart," the person sitting next to her interjected. "If you have a couple of minutes after this meeting, I'll show you."

This solved the woman's problem, so we moved on to the next idea. As we continued down the list, a pattern emerged. Many of the ideas involved throwing large amounts of money at problems that could be addressed more effectively and inexpensively with a little thought and creativity. (Unsophisticated problem-solvers often do this.) To illustrate the lesson that money and resourcefulness offset each other, we went back to the first idea.

"Clearly the office will run more efficiently if everyone knows more about Excel. But you can't justify $15,000 on Excel training. Suppose you had only $50. What could you do?" Ruling out the expensive solution is a facilitation "trick" that forced the group to think more creatively.

Based on the exchange between the two women in the back, it didn't take long for the group to come up with a much better solution than "Excel training for everyone." In an office of thirty users of Microsoft Office, chances are that someone has the answer to almost any question about it. Why not put up a bulletin board (cost: $25) for questions people have about any of the Microsoft Office suite? Or why not identify several "power users" in the office as "go-to" people for questions? By going back to the underlying problem and ruling out the possibility of throwing money at it, the group developed a set of inexpensive ideas that solved it elegantly and much more effectively than two days of offsite training would have.

Most supervisors will need some coaching to hone their facilitation skills. One way to do this is to have higher-level managers regularly attend idea meetings in their areas of responsibility. They can observe their supervisors in action and coach them. Particularly in the beginning, it is helpful to make structured feedback an integral part of these visits to ensure that the coaching is done in a consistent and effective manner. Formalized feedback can be as simple as filling out a short form stating what the supervisor/facilitator did well and how he or she could improve; the form should be completed by the observer during the meeting and discussed with the supervisor immediately afterward.

ESCALATION

Sometimes decisions about ideas cannot be made on the front lines and will need to be escalated to higher levels. The ideas may require resources that are not available to the front-line teams (such as skills, time, and/or money), may require the involvement of other departments or functions, may require dedicated problem-solving resources (such as Six Sigma projects, *kaizen* events, or R&D initiatives), or may simply involve issues that require higher-level scrutiny or permission.

The escalation process should be rapid and transparent, clearly define how the various types of ideas will be routed, and articulate the decision-making authorities and expectations for follow-through at each level. When no clear escalation process exists, ideas are handled in an ad hoc manner and can easily get lost or stalled. Whenever escalated ideas are not promptly addressed, employee trust in the system erodes.

The escalation process at Scania, the Swedish truck maker whose system we discussed earlier, has all of the necessary attributes. At the end of each front-line team's weekly idea meeting, the team leader puts escalated ideas on his or her *supervisor's* board for consideration at that person's weekly meeting with all his or her team leaders. If the supervisor's idea meeting decides that an idea needs to be escalated further, it goes to the *line manager's* board, and from there, if needed, to the leadership team's board. Because the boards at each level are visible to everyone, front-line workers can follow the progress of an escalated idea all the way up the chain of command.

At Scania, most escalated ideas are dealt with in a week or two. But some may need more investigation or coordination among groups, and still others may have to wait until the next budgeting cycle. For example, one idea in the diesel engine assembly plant outside Stockholm had to do with the workstation instruction-sheet packets that traveled with each engine through the plant. Scania's engines are custom-made, so every workstation needs specific assembly instructions for every engine. The idea was to replace the physical packets of documentation with flat-panel screens mounted on the conveyor carriages used to transport the engines from station to station. With the appropriate processing information displayed on the screen as the engine arrived at each station, an enormous amount of paperwork would be eliminated, documents would no longer get misplaced, and time would be saved since the workers would no longer need to shuffle through paperwork for their instructions. Because the idea had plantwide implications and would require a large investment, it was escalated all the way up to the leadership team. There, it was parked until it could be considered in the next year's capital budgeting process, where it was approved. Although it took some time to approve and implement the idea, the important thing was that the front-line team members who came up with it knew exactly what was happening with it every step of the way.

An important rule in escalation is that before an idea can be escalated to the next level, all the research and support work that can be done for it at the lower levels needs to have been done. Borrowing a term from the British Army, we refer to this requirement as the need for "completed staff work." Keeping staff work as low in the organization as possible allows more ideas to be handled faster and at a lower cost.

Ideas that are escalated with poor or incomplete staff work represent coaching opportunities. Not only should the ideas be sent back down for further work, but the reasons that the staff work was deficient should be clearly explained. If this is done consistently, over time team members will come to understand the kinds of information that upper managers need to make their decisions and will learn how to make stronger cases for ideas. Teams will then prefilter their own ideas, and decisions on the ideas they do escalate will be much easier and usually positive. As Larry Acquarulo, CEO of Foster Corporation, a medium-sized, Connecticut-based medical products company, observed after revamping his escalation process to require completed staff work:

> It used to be that I would get all kinds of ideas, many of them half-baked, that I would have to check out myself. It wasted a lot of my time. Now I have become largely a rubber stamp.

In a similar vein, when ideas are escalated that should have been decided on at a lower level, it indicates that people may be uncertain about their responsibilities and levels of authority. We encountered such a situation during the pilot phase at the Big Y supermarket chain discussed in Chapter 2. A checkout clerk at one of the stores suggested that signs be put up in the parking lot to remind people to bring in their eco-bags. He had noticed that customers would often express embarrassment to him about forgetting to bring in their reusable eco-bags. His team liked the idea and forwarded it to the store director. This director, who had been with the company only a couple of months, also liked the idea and immediately escalated it to his boss, the district director. The district director also thought that it was a good idea, but because a store's parking lot was the store director's responsibility, he assumed the store director was taking care of it and took no action. However, after three weeks, the tracking software flagged the idea as stalled due to the district director's inaction, and it was highlighted for review at the next senior management meeting. In the ensuing discussion, the group confirmed that the idea should have been implemented by the store director, and that the incident provided an excellent opportunity for the district director to talk with his new store director about his authority and responsibilities.

Many organizations also use their escalation processes to *replicate* ideas that can be used elsewhere in the organization. While the eco-bag sign idea was not escalated for this purpose, it did bring the idea to the attention of top management, who then made sure it was implemented systemwide. And when it was used in all of Big Y's sixty stores, its value was greatly multiplied.

One final note on escalation: it is important to link your front-line idea system with the other improvement and innovation systems in your organization, such as lean, Six Sigma, quality improvement, and product development or R&D. Many of these links should be designed into the escalation process. We will discuss this topic more in Chapters 6 and 8.

THE ELECTRONIC SUGGESTION BOX TRAP

It is important not to confuse high-performance idea processes with traditional suggestion systems. Almost every organization of any size has tried, at one time or another, to set up some kind of system to collect employee suggestions. Although today's suggestion systems are generally online, almost all of them are based on suggestion box thinking, and they handle ideas in exactly the same way as a nineteenth-century suggestion box process. Automating the process does not get away from its intrinsic limitations. You can put lipstick on a pig, but it is still a pig.

To avoid the mistake of setting up a glorified suggestion box process, it is vital to understand why such processes are fundamentally flawed.

The basic suggestion box process is as follows. Employees submit suggestions to defined collection points. Each suggestion is given an initial review and routed to an appropriate manager, subject-matter expert, or committee for evaluation. This person's or committee's recommendation is then sent to a decision maker, or sometimes a decision-making committee. If the suggestion is accepted, it is assigned to someone to implement. If it is rejected, the suggester is sent a nice note with some kind of explanation. Electronic suggestion boxes merely automate the submission, routing, tracking, and notification components.

Standard complaints about suggestion box–type processes include the following:

- They get very few ideas, most of which are of questionable quality.
- They are bureaucratic, slow, and biased toward rejecting ideas.
- The results obtained are rarely worth the time, hassle, and overhead of running the system.

Armed with an understanding of how high-performing systems work, it is easy to see the reasons for the deficiencies of suggestion boxes.

The quantity and quality of ideas are low because the suggestion box process generally collects suggestions made by *individuals* from their own *limited perspectives*. The quantity is low because the suggestion box process is voluntary and not integrated into regular work, there is little accountability for managerial follow-through, front-line workers aren't empowered to take initiative, and the process is limited to solutions and does not accept problems. The quality of suggestions is low because they do not have the benefit of being vetted by colleagues who discuss the underlying problems and consider possible alternative solutions. Furthermore, the suggestion box process does not focus people on the organization's strategic goals, so most of the suggestions are of limited value.

Suggestion systems are slow and bureaucratic because of problems with how ideas are evaluated. Since the task of evaluating ideas is usually assigned to managers in addition to their regular work, it gets a low priority and responses are slow in coming. And when an idea is approved, implementing it becomes extra work for someone else who is also already busy.

What is more, the evaluation is usually done at some distance from the front lines, often by a person who has little understanding of the context of the idea, feels little urgency about the underlying problem, and has little time to spare. (We have come across cases where the evaluator was literally *thousands of miles* away from the situation involved.) To be confident in approving an idea, this distant evaluator needs more information and time to become familiar with the situation involved. But time pressure, combined with the risk involved in approving a bad idea, means *rejecting* an idea is safer than accepting it. After all, approving it means the evaluator accepts some responsibility if it fails. Rejecting it means doing nothing, which will not make anything worse. All this creates a strong bias for *rejection.*

In short, suggestion box–type processes are gigantic doom loops. Their voluntary nature means employees are going beyond their job descriptions to give in ideas. The poorly designed process means that the ideas are usually not of very high quality and represent extra work for the evaluators, who find it easier and safer to reject them. So employees lose interest and give in fewer ideas. When management doesn't see many good ideas coming in, it thinks that employees don't really have many good ideas and so gives the system even less support. The system spirals down into relative or even total oblivion.

It would be hard to come up with a plausible process that is better designed to shut down ideas than a suggestion box–type process. In many ways, having such a process is worse than having no process at all.

KEY POINTS

✓ There are three archetypes of high-performing idea processes:

- ☐ *Kaizen teian* systems, the first generation of high-performing processes, are essentially suggestion systems that have been highly streamlined to mitigate their inherent processing problems and turbocharged with a strong culture of improvement.

- ☐ In the *idea meeting* process, people bring "opportunities for improvement" to their regular team or department meetings, where they are discussed and implementation actions are decided.

- ☐ The *idea board* process also has regular idea meetings but incorporates a large visible board to help collect and process ideas. The board's highly visual nature helps keep ideas front-of-mind on a daily basis and creates social pressure to complete assigned tasks on time. It also allows higher-level managers and colleagues to see instantly how active each idea team is and its current improvement projects.

✓ Take a problem-focused perspective with ideas. Often the person who identifies a problem is not the right person to solve it, and even when a solution is offered, it frequently pays to go back to the underlying problem to explore alternative approaches.

✓ Sometimes decisions about ideas cannot be made on the front lines and will need to be escalated to higher levels. The escalation process should be rapid and transparent, clearly define how the various types of ideas are routed, and articulate the decision-making authorities and expectations for follow-through at each level.

✓ High-performance idea processes are completely different from traditional suggestion systems. Although today's suggestion systems are generally online, they handle ideas in exactly the same way as a nineteenth-century suggestion box process. Automating the process does not get away from its intrinsic limitations.

6

Implementing a
High-Performing
Idea System

SEVERAL YEARS AGO, a vice president at a Fortune 500 financial services company approached us to help her set up a high-performing idea system. She was in a hurry and asked if it was possible to get the pilot areas started in two months and begin rolling the system out a few months later. We explained that it was certainly doable but would require the creation of a strong design and implementation team, whose members would have to be able to do a lot of work in a short period of time. The effort would also inevitably require her to champion some organization-level changes to the leadership team. She agreed and recruited the team, and we set to work.

During the initial training sessions, the design team members began to appreciate the scale and scope of what they were being asked to do. Unfortunately, the vice president skipped out on those training sessions after the first hour, so she never really understood what designing and launching the new system would involve. She soon began pushing up the launch dates, insisting on unrealistic deadlines, and dismissing the team's advice and requests. At what turned out to be our last meeting with the design team, its members were very disheartened and felt betrayed by that

VP. Shortly thereafter, the team's leader left the company, and the effort disintegrated.

The mistake this vice president made was to assume that setting up an idea system was relatively straightforward, simply a matter of layering a collection and evaluation process on top of the existing organization. Unfortunately, this is a common assumption. But launching an idea system without properly preparing both the organization and its people usually dooms the initiative to failure.

This chapter is a step-by-step guide to implementing a high-performing idea system. It is based on what we have learned over the last two decades from studying, watching, and participating firsthand in both successful and failed launches. The implementation process we recommend has the following nine steps:

Step 1. Ensure the leadership's long-term commitment to the new idea system.

Step 2. Form and train the team that will design and implement the system.

Step 3. Assess the organization from an idea management perspective.

Step 4. Design the idea system.

Step 5. Start correcting misalignments.

Step 6. Conduct a pilot test.

Step 7. Assess the pilot results, make adjustments, and prepare for the launch.

Step 8. Roll out the system organization-wide.

Step 9. Continue to improve the system.

How long each of these steps take depends on the size and complexity of the organization and the overall sense of urgency. A small and simple organization can get a system up and fully deployed in less than six months, whereas a large global organization may need a couple of years or more, depending on the resources committed to the initiative.

STEP 1
Ensure the Leadership's Long-term Commitment to the New Idea System

When a leadership team sees an idea system as an important capability-building initiative, its members are more likely to have the patience and perseverance to provide the long-term leadership needed to deploy the system in a strategic manner.

Consider how the high-performing idea system at Alpha Natural Resources ("Alpha" for short), the second-largest coal-mining company in the United States, gave it a unique capability that was an important element in making a major strategic acquisition.

On April 5, 2010, an explosion at the Massey Energy Company's Upper Big Branch coal mine resulted in the deaths of twenty-nine miners. These were not the first deaths in Massey's mines. The company had one of the worst safety records in the industry and was constantly in conflict with the Federal Mine Safety and Health Administration (MSHA). The backlash and lawsuits from the disaster suddenly put the ongoing viability of Massey into question. In June 2011, Alpha, a mining company of approximately its same size, stepped in and acquired Massey.

Although both companies used similar equipment and technologies, the way they dealt with their employees was vastly different. Massey was highly autocratic, whereas Alpha put a great deal of emphasis on listening to its employees and getting their ideas. Since its founding in 2002, Alpha's guiding principles were incorporated into what it called its "Running Right" philosophy, which focused on the importance of the front-line miner. The Running Right idea system had been started with a focus on safety but grew to include front-line ideas on productivity and other areas as well. Instead of having Massey's management-dictated approach to safety, Alpha involved its miners in identifying safety problems and coming up with ideas to address them. As the system took hold, Alpha noticed that the more ideas per miner a mine got, the fewer safety problems it had.

For Alpha's CEO Kevin Crutchfield and the members of his leadership team, running safe mines was a fundamental value and vital to the company's long-term success. Having all been former miners themselves, they had firsthand knowledge of the inherent dangers in mining. Studies by Alpha showed that 88 percent of safety incidents were due to unsafe behavior on the part of the miners, not to deficiencies in equipment, technologies, or safety policies. And the best way to get safe behavior, Alpha's leadership reasoned, was not through top-down edicts, but by listening to the miners' safety concerns and rapidly acting on their ideas. After all, the miners paid a steep price for poor safety. Alpha's leaders never questioned the time, effort, and resources needed to make their idea system successful.

Soon after Alpha acquired Massey Energy, it moved aggressively to integrate the Running Right idea system and the Alpha culture into every one of the former Massey mines. Each mine was shut down for a day of training in order to assure that the miners learned about the Running Right philosophy, why this philosophy was important to them and the company, and how the idea system worked. A member of Alpha's leadership team attended each mine's training day to personally commit the company to acting on the miners' ideas. The commitment shown by Alpha's leadership in shutting down the mines for this training was not missed by the miners. It was inconceivable that their former bosses would have stopped production for training, much less an entire day of it!

A second early move by Alpha's leaders was to hold a two-day "Leadership Summit" for the company's 220 top managers—roughly half of whom came from Massey. For longtime Alpha managers, the summit was a chance to work on what the Running Right philosophy meant for the future; for former Massey managers, it was an introduction to an entirely new way of managing. CEO Crutchfield framed the importance of the company's front-line focus in a poignant way: When all the company's top managers were attending the summit, every mine continued to operate normally; but when the miners were being trained, all production stopped. The front-line miners, not management, Crutchfield emphasized, were the people most critical to the company's success.

The investment paid off. Within *five months* of the acquisition, a number of the former Massey mines had reached or exceeded Alpha's average number of ideas per miner, and their safety performance had improved dramatically. The leadership team then proceeded to develop a *five-year* plan to keep improving the idea system's performance so it could continue to deliver major strategic advantages. (Disclosure: one of the authors advised the company during this process.)

The success of Alpha's acquisition of Massey depended on rapidly fixing Massey's safety problems, which would have been very difficult without the Running Right idea system and Alpha's leaders' quick action to integrate it into the newly acquired company.

When considering whether to launch a high-performing idea system, the first question that needs to be asked is why. What are the key strategic capabilities that the organization wants from the initiative? In the case of Alpha, its leaders knew that mine safety was critical for the company's success, and set up its idea system with this in mind. From there, it grew into providing additional strategic capabilities.

STEP 2
Form and Train the Team That Will Design and Implement the System

As we have said before, a high-performing idea system has to be designed so it can be integrated into the way the organization already works. Step 2 is to form and train a team that has the power, credibility, and collective knowledge to design such an integrated system, to address the potentially significant organizational issues that will inevitably arise, and to lead the launch organization-wide.

To see how this works, consider how Health New England (HNE), a medium-sized health care insurance company, put together its seven-member team to design and oversee the implementation of its idea system. The team comprised

- the company's well-respected IT director as its leader;
- the company's general counsel and a member of the Executive Leadership Team (ELT), who volunteered to be the executive champion;
- four middle managers, one each from operations, sales, marketing, and technology; and
- a front-line employee who was known for constantly proposing improvement ideas.

Note the composition of this design team. First, it had a respected upper middle manager as leader. Second, it included a member of the ELT to provide top management's perspective, help the team navigate sensitive issues, and promote the idea system at the highest level. Some of the team's recommendations would require modifications in corporate-level policies and practices, or commitments of corporate-level resources. The ELT member was able to provide an executive perspective and offer critical advice, such as "It might be best to say this in a different way" or "Some members of the ELT might have a problem with this for the following reasons." He also acted as a conduit for information between the team and the ELT.

Third, the team included a cadre of middle managers, who represented an important constituency that would be critical for the success of the new system. Finally, the front-line employee brought a perspective to the team that the other members lacked. For example, during a discussion of how much time employees would be given to work on improvement ideas, and how this time would be allocated, one of the managers commented that he thought supervisors would be very supportive of freeing their people's time to work on ideas. After all, he reasoned, these ideas would improve their units. But the front-line employee said, "With respect, the situation in the work centers is actually quite different from what you imagine. Supervisors are under a lot of pressure to service the customers in a timely fashion. Just today, my supervisor told me that we had so many claims to process that she was reluctant to let me attend this meeting. I will have to somehow make up the work later today. My biggest concern is that supervisors won't support the system. They will see it as interfering with the work that has to get done." This point led to a discussion of staffing issues, the need for more training and coaching support for the supervisors, and the importance of holding supervisors and managers accountable for ideas. The team also realized that CEO Peter Straley would have to communicate strongly to the supervisors that ideas were a priority, and it was now company policy that employees were to be given release time to work on them.

Once the design team is assembled, it must be provided with a thorough education in idea management. Its members will need to have a strong understanding of what high-performing idea processes look like, how they work, and how to address the challenges they will face in creating one. The initial training can involve classes taught by experts, reading relevant books, and perhaps visits to idea-driven organizations. For the HNE team, the process began with a day of training in idea systems, and then reading and studying two books on managing ideas.

Once the team began to apply its new knowledge, it began to learn by doing, starting with the assessment of HNE from an ideas perspective (see Step 3). As the team members interviewed front-line employees, supervisors, and middle and upper managers, they discovered impediments to the flow of ideas that needed to be addressed. This "action learning" continued as the team designed their system and rolled it out through their company. In the end, the members of the design team developed considerable expertise in the management of ideas, and HNE went on to successfully implement a high-performing idea system.

If you take care to choose the right people for your design team, and then provide them with the training and time they need to do their job well, you will be setting your new idea system up for success.

STEP 3
Assess the Organization from an
Idea Management Perspective

The assessment has two purposes. First, it must identify misalignments and any potential challenges to implementing the idea initiative. Second, it should try to find opportunities to integrate the idea system into the organization's existing systems. The assessment typically includes interviews with front-line workers, supervisors, and managers to discover what might hinder the flow of ideas and what might help it. Here are some typical lines of inquiry:

- Have the interviewees been involved in implementing any ideas or improvements in the past in the organization? If so, what were the challenges they faced and what helped them along the way?
- How easy is it for employees and supervisors to get the resources and support they need to implement their ideas?

- What other mechanisms for bottom-up ideas does the organization have? How well do these work, and what, if any, are the problems with them?
- Have there been any failed idea initiatives in the past? Why did they fail, and what are the implications of their failures for the new initiative?
- How can existing practices and forums—such as annual evaluations, bonuses, reporting systems, newsletters, CEO e-mails, corporate videos, regular meetings—be used to support the idea initiative?
- Does the culture, and the way people are evaluated and rewarded, support innovative behavior? What changes, if any, are needed in these areas?
- What problems, if any, might keep the upcoming idea system from being successful?

Some of the issues that assessments uncover are relatively easy to fix, such as adding a modest budget to allow teams to make purchases to implement small ideas, retasking support departments to provide help with implementing ideas, or amending policies to increase the decision-making authority of people at lower levels. But assessments almost always flag more fundamental concerns as well. Take, for example, the issues we identified from an assessment of an international division of a Fortune 500 food and beverage company (sample supporting comments from interviewees are in italics):

- Past leadership behavior was creating serious concern that top management would only support the idea initiative and not provide the active leadership it would need.
  - □ *My biggest fear is that top management will pay only lip service to this [the idea system] and not realize that it will require work from them, too.*
  - □ *To be successful, this initiative really must come from the top and be led by the top.*

- Top management's overdependence on the numbers when making decisions was creating a lot of non-value-adding work and leading to some poor decisions.

□ *One new product was clearly terrible. All thirty members of its marketing team agreed that it was a disaster. Yet we still had to spend several months and $40,000 to prove it to top management.*

□ *Innovation can dilute margins in the short term, and if you don't hit your quarterly numbers, you are dead here.*

□ *We focus on costs and budgets so much that it is usually much easier <u>not</u> to do anything new.*

■ The company does not have a culture of innovation. "Innovations" are limited to minor line extensions and packaging changes.

□ *This company kills anything that has a germ of innovativeness in it. We require too much analysis and make people jump through too many hoops.*

□ *We need to carve out time for innovation, and not have it be just an add-on.*

□ *We are told it's OK to fail, but it isn't, really.*

None of these issues came as a complete surprise to anyone. But when the design team brought the documented list of them to the leadership team, the problems could no longer be ignored.

A tactic we use to elicit deeper conversations among the design team members about the issues the team needs to face is the *pre-mortem*: "Suppose we were to get in a time machine and go forward three years, and you were to learn that the idea initiative had failed. Why would this have happened?" This question usually surfaces some "brutal facts" that would otherwise stay buried.

Another purpose of the assessment is to identify potential opportunities to integrate the idea system into existing management systems, and how these, in turn, might be adapted to support the needs of the idea system. This is an application of the principle of "minimal intervention"; that is, whenever doing something new in an organization, it is much better, wherever possible, to take advantage of what is already being done instead of creating entirely new mechanisms. Existing systems, policies, and practices incorporate a great deal of previous learning. Building on them takes advantage of this learning while reducing the risk of introducing new problems. In addition, it is more effective and respectful of people to fit the necessary changes into their existing work routines as much as possible. The principle of minimal intervention encourages this integration, makes adapting to the new system easier, and reduces resistance to it.

Some examples of the questions we use to identify these minimally intervening opportunities are as follows:

- Can idea meetings be integrated into regular department meetings?
- Can idea performance be incorporated into existing review processes for both workers and managers? What about the merit, bonus, and promotion processes?
- Can idea system training be incorporated into new employee orientation? Can idea activator training modules (discussed in Chapter 7) be incorporated into the organization's existing training matrix? Are there any existing training modules that could be tweaked into idea activators?
- Are there existing communication forums, such as corporate newsletters or Internet portals, that can be used to support the idea initiative?
- How can the idea system help, and be helped by, existing improvement and innovation efforts—such as Six Sigma, lean, innovation centers, or new product development?

The more completely the idea system can be integrated into existing practices and procedures, and the fewer new practices and procedures are created especially for it, the more easily and quickly it will become accepted as a regular part of the way the company works, and the better it will perform.

By the end of the assessment step, you will not have a complete inventory of every misalignment and integration opportunity. However, you should have identified the major misalignments that you need to correct before you start, as well as some integration opportunities that will make the idea system easier to deploy and more readily accepted by the organization. As we have previously discussed, removing misalignments is an ongoing process that never ends. The same is true of discovering and creating new integration opportunities.

STEP 4
Design the Idea System

As Oliver Wendell Holmes once put it:

I would not give a fig for the simplicity this side of complexity, but I would give my life for the simplicity on the other side of complexity.

Many design teams begin their work thinking that it will be simple—all they will need to do is to set up a process to collect ideas from front-line employees. But by the end of their training and the assessment, almost every design team feels overwhelmed by the complexity of setting up a major new management system whose implications cut across the entire organization. The team's goal—which can be very challenging—is to come up with a simple system that successfully addresses all this complexity. The system has to be simple in order to handle large numbers of ideas efficiently.

To push design teams to attain the necessary simplicity, we like to ask them—even in large organizations—to come up with a document of no more than five pages laying out the entire system. To do this, the team members will have to address a number of issues about the mechanics of the new system and how it will be managed and led, such as these:

- Who will be responsible for overseeing the system?
- What will the mechanics of the idea process look like? That is:
  - How will ideas be collected, processed, and implemented at the front-line level?
  - What levels of authority are needed to implement which kinds of ideas?
  - What budgets and resources will each level have access to?
  - What will the escalation process look like?
  - How will the process integrate with other problem-solving and improvement mechanisms?
  - How will good ideas be replicated?
- What metrics will be used to measure idea performance and how will managers and employees be held accountable for them?

- Will the company offer recognition to employees and/or managers? If so, how?
- What is the role of middle managers and senior executives in the idea system? What will be their new "leader standard work" (discussed in Chapter 2) to support ideas?
- What initial and ongoing training will be given to employees, supervisors, managers, and the leadership team?
- How will the performance of the idea system itself be evaluated and improved?

STEP 5
Start Correcting Misalignments

It is impossible, and also unnecessary, to align your organization perfectly before launching your idea system. As we discussed in Chapters 3 and 4, the process of alignment takes time, and maintaining and improving it will be an ongoing effort.

The true nature and full ramifications of some misalignments will become clear only after the system launches. Others will be clear from the outset, but dealing with them will need to be deferred for practical or political reasons, or because fully correcting them will require more time than is available. But before the launch, it is important to eliminate any misalignments that are going to seriously hinder the implementation of front-line ideas.

Recall, for example, that large national retailer where front-line supervisors and managers were forwarding even the smallest decisions to their bosses. Senior executives complained to us about the number of low-level decisions requiring their approval. In one case, a straightforward request for a whiteboard marker had gone up through four levels of management until it landed on the desk of the vice president for purchasing. Such ridiculous misalignments in decision-making authorities had to be corrected before the launch, or making even the most obvious small improvements would be painful. The supervisors' spending authority was increased significantly, and each department was given a modest budget for purchasing supplies for small improvements.

But a related, more delicate misalignment needed to be dealt with more diplomatically. Several members of the leadership team believed that while the company should move in the direction of a more empowering culture, pushing too far too fast would be imprudent. So the leadership adopted a go-slow approach. At first, the idea system would focus on small ideas at the departmental level. Cross-functional ideas would be handled at the discretion of the managers involved, using existing or informal channels. Vice presidents who wanted to move faster could encourage their managers to take more initiative on bigger or more cross-functional problems, and the vice presidents who wanted to go slower could do so.

STEP 6
Conduct a Pilot Test

A pilot test is a small-scale live test of the idea system before it is rolled out to the entire organization. For larger organizations, it typically involves running the idea system in a small set of departments or teams (typically, three to five). In small organizations—say, those with less than forty people—the pilot test may involve everyone and simply be a designated time frame of experimentation and learning after the idea system is started up, but before it is considered to be "officially" launched.

From time to time, we encounter impatient leaders who insist on launching their idea initiatives without a pilot test. While omitting or shortcutting the pilot might appear to get the idea initiative off to a faster start, doing so will dramatically slow things down later. Problems will go undiscovered that will become increasingly disruptive and difficult to correct when the system is broadly deployed. Also, opportunities to enhance the system's performance and increase its acceptance across the organization will be lost.

For example, a few years ago, the leadership of a U.S. military base was anticipating severe budget cuts. Eager to find cost savings while also meeting increasingly demanding service requirements, the base's leadership launched its idea system without a meaningful pilot test. Nine months later, only 25 percent of the idea teams were functioning well. A major reason for this shortfall was that the training for supervisors had been limited to a mandatory viewing of a fifteen-minute video explaining the process. This video, though well intentioned, had been rushed into production. It was uninspiring, factually incorrect about the process, and contained a great deal of bad advice. As a result, more than a hundred front-line managers had been running painfully unproductive idea meetings for months, and significant resentment toward the idea system had developed throughout the base. A well-executed pilot step would have detected and fixed the problematic training before it created the much bigger problem that required considerable leadership time and energy to correct. As it was, the system struggled for almost two years before gaining any real traction.

A pilot test should

- provide a small-scale *live test* of the idea system to identify opportunities to make it better,
- generate *evidence of the value* of the system that can be used to build support for it,
- *develop a cadre of coaches and champions* experienced in managing ideas to support the new system as it rolls out across the organization, and
- help *replace uncertainty* about the new initiative *with anticipation.*

Live Test. The launch of an idea system introduces many changes across the organization, the full ramifications of which are impossible to predict. The pilot provides an opportunity to identify any resulting problems and fix them before they can do much damage. It allows people to point out these problems without the risk of being viewed as complainers. The status of "pilot" also gives a license to experiment and to make even substantial changes to the initial design without anyone losing credibility or being embarrassed. In this way, the pilot is a safety zone.

Even when significant problems have been identified through the assessment (Step 3), sometimes decision makers need more evidence before being willing to tackle them. For example, at a large European insurance company, the assessment had predicted that the limited IT support for employee ideas would create a bottleneck, but management was reluctant to dedicate more IT resources prior to the pilot. However, when the CEO and CIO (chief information officer) were shown a list of the ideas from the pilot that had been put on hold as a result, along with estimates of the opportunity costs of each week's delay in implementing them, the CIO immediately reassigned a small team to support the idea system.

Problems with training, linkages with other systems and processes, resourcing, and behavior are recurring themes in the pilot phase. But because these are often situation-specific, they can be difficult to see or solve until the ideas start coming in and the exact nature of the problems is understood.

Evidence of Value. It is always useful to develop early evidence of the value of the idea system. Almost every organization has some managers who have previously had bad experiences with suggestion box–type systems or other poorly conceived idea initiatives, and who naturally have reservations about the value of the new idea system. Our favorite method to start addressing these reservations is to provide these managers with a list of front-line ideas implemented during the pilot, as we did for the CEO of the insurance company described earlier. Such a list also helps reduce any concern or hesitation on the part of the employees, as it demonstrates that the ideas coming in are not only nonthreatening, but helpful.

Develops a Cadre of Coaches and Champions. By the end of the pilot at STCC (the community college discussed in the last chapter), the supervisors in charge of each of the three pilot teams had become very proficient at managing ideas. The counsel of this small cadre of experts proved invaluable. During the college-wide rollout of the idea system, this trio volunteered to attend meetings in the newly launched areas to provide coaching, and they invited supervisors in these areas to observe their own meetings. One issue they helped with, for example, was that some of the more recently promoted supervisors were still feeling out their roles, and their people's ideas were frequently putting them in situations where they were unsure of their responsibilities and authority. Did they *have* to accept all the ideas their team voted to do, even the ones they disagreed with? Was it appropriate for their subordinates to approach other supervisors, without their being present, if they needed information or help with ideas? And what happens when a team wants to work on an idea, but the supervisor has sensitive information he or she cannot share that is relevant to how well the idea will work? The members of the cadre, who had wrestled with these kinds of issues themselves, had both the legitimacy and experience needed to help the new supervisors work through them.

Replacing Uncertainty with Anticipation. When the decision to launch an idea system is announced, typically everyone has a lot of questions and concerns: "How will it affect my job?" "How much time will it take, and how can I find that time?" "How can I come up with all the ideas expected of me?" "Is the effort really worthwhile?"

A successful pilot test turns these concerns into a positive anticipation by answering these questions and demonstrating the benefits of front-line ideas. At the national retailer we discussed in Step 5, when workers in other departments saw their colleagues in the pilot areas using their new idea systems and spending authority to eliminate long-standing annoyances, they began pestering their managers about when they could start to work on their problems, too.

Organizing the Pilot

To fulfill its purpose, a pilot has to be successful both from the technical perspective and the management-of-change perspective. That is, it has to verify that the idea system design basically works, and it has to demonstrate the advantages of the system. If the design team has done its job, technical success should be straightforward. Consequently, the overriding consideration becomes demonstrating the system's value.

The critical design questions for the pilot are as follows:

- Which areas should be selected for the pilot test?
- What kind of training and support should be provided to pilot-area supervisors and employees?
- How long will the pilot last?

A key consideration in selecting pilot areas is their managers' leadership skills and enthusiasm for the initiative. The single-biggest factor in making a pilot area successful is the quality of its manager. The pilot test is not a time to work with difficult managers, troubled teams, or areas with logistical issues that would add to the challenges of starting an idea process. The time to tackle challenging areas is *after* the organization has developed expertise in idea management.

Once the pilot areas are selected, their managers need to receive training as well as plenty of support and coaching. The certification program we described in Chapter 2 is a good example of what this might include.

The pilot period is generally three or four months long. People need enough time to learn their new roles, enough ideas need to be processed to give the system a realistic "stress" test, and enough ideas need to be implemented to demonstrate the value of the system.

Make Corrections While the Pilot Is Still Running

It is important not to wait until the pilot test is over to review performance and make changes. The earlier that problems are identified and action is taken, the better the results of the pilot test will be.

The trick to rapid problem identification is getting good information in a timely fashion. Design team members and managers should observe idea meetings and interact with the people in the pilot areas. Everyone in these areas should be encouraged to "yell loudly" when they become aware of system-related problems. In addition, pilot area supervisors should meet regularly with the design team to discuss issues and concerns.

The insights gained through these interactions will help the design team understand what is driving the quantitative data it collects. Such data typically includes the numbers of implemented ideas in each area, how many escalated ideas have been forwarded to whom, and how many have been responded to in a timely manner. To provide quantitative data in near real time, some organizations develop highly visual "dashboards"— typically driven by web-based programs that draw information directly from the databases used to record and manage ideas. Dashboards allow managers to easily monitor how ideas are flowing, analyze patterns, and quickly identify problems. Taken together, the qualitative and quantitative information gives the design team a holistic view of the system and allows them to quickly flag areas that need help.

For example, during the three-month pilot test at the large national retail chain we discussed earlier, the pilot area supervisors were encouraged to complain whenever they experienced problems or bottlenecks, and to propose system improvements. To make this process as easy as possible, every week each pilot area supervisor and his or her manager met with a member of the idea staff to talk about opportunities to improve the system. In addition, once a month, the idea staff organized a one-hour meeting with all the pilot area supervisors and their managers so they could share experiences, discuss tactics and problems, and swap solutions. In the first meeting, several items came to light and were quickly resolved:

- Supervisors reported that ideas requiring even modest purchases were getting backlogged in the procurement process. The VP of human resources, who was also the idea system's executive champion, met with the head of purchasing, who agreed to initiate a fast-track purchasing process for front-line ideas and to staff it with an energetic purchasing agent instructed to help the pilot departments in any way she could.
- It became apparent that the supervisors' idea facilitation skills were weak. Within a week, a training/coaching program was developed and delivered to each supervisor on an individual basis.
- Because the front-line teams turned out to be much more responsible with their budgets than management expected, their spending limit was raised from $25 to $250 per idea.

As we mentioned earlier, the status of "pilot" confers a license to suspend normal operating rules and to make changes to the idea system, and to the management systems, while the pilot is still underway. As evidence begins to accumulate that certain policies or procedures are hindering ideas, top managers are often willing to suspend or allow temporary workarounds to them during the pilot period. Such changes are generally low-risk given that they will automatically expire with the completion of the pilot test. But if they do prove effective, it is then much easier to make the case for a permanent change.

STEP 7
Assess the Pilot Results, Make Adjustments, and Prepare for the Launch

Once the pilot has been completed, a full review of it should be conducted with the intent to

- Identify any problems with the idea-handling process, including those caused by misalignments in the organization's management systems.
- Determine whether additional resources are needed in any critical areas.
- Capture "lessons learned" that will help with the organization-wide rollout.

Many of the issues identified in the review, such as training shortfalls or glitches in the mechanics of the idea process, will be solvable by the design team. But some issues will require senior management involvement. Two of the more common ones are (1) difficulties with the escalation process and (2) decision-making processes that are cumbersome, inappropriate, or flawed.

Few organizations have systems in place to effectively handle ideas escalated from the front lines. Until managers experience the challenges involved, it can be hard for them to get their minds around how their escalation process should work. Recall that ideas are escalated for three reasons: (1) they need permission from higher levels; (2) they need more resources than are available to front-line teams; or (3) they are cross-functional—that is, they require the involvement of different areas of the organization. Ideas escalated for either of the first two reasons can usually be handled through the existing chain of command. But cross-functional ideas originating from the front-lines are a different story.

While almost all organizations have experience working with cross-functional ideas, this experience is typically with ideas that come down from higher up in the organization. They usually address larger issues and are handled either through regular management meetings, by special ad hoc project teams, or with informal manager-to-manager interactions.

Such approaches are impractical for handling large numbers of (generally smaller) bottom-up cross-functional ideas addressing problems on the front lines that are not so visible to management. These kinds of ideas need streamlined mechanisms capable of handling them quickly and efficiently. Because an escalation process will define how senior managers will interact with bottom-up ideas, senior managers need to be directly involved in its design.

A second issue that often requires senior management attention is when decision-making processes are too cumbersome, inappropriate, or flawed to handle large numbers of bottom-up ideas. Proposed improvements may require too many approvals, approvals at too high a level, or approvals from the wrong people. Rationalizing these kinds of decision-making problems may require some political wrangling, but conceptually they are simple to correct.

A decision-making problem that is more challenging to address is when management puts too much emphasis on the numbers and requires detailed cost-benefit analyses (CBAs) for even the most obvious ideas. As we discussed in Chapter 2, CBA is a poor decision-making tool in most situations because it is inherently inaccurate. Furthermore, insisting on CBA as the default decision-making tool merely creates a lot of non-value-adding work for front-line employees. Because this institutional mindset typically comes from the top, it typically has to be changed by the top, too. A good way to start is to present senior managers with strong evidence that too much emphasis on CBA is actually costing them money by blocking profitable ideas.

For example, during the assessment phase at a financial services company, many people warned us that the leadership's myopic focus on the numbers was blocking the flow of ideas. For example, a secretary in accounts receivable told us that the company was printing the wrong return mail address on its invoices, causing hundreds of checks per week to go to the wrong office some twenty miles away across a major city. But she couldn't get the problem corrected without doing a thorough CBA to prove that the money saved would justify the expense of the change. Because she didn't know how to do this, she dropped the idea. She brought it up again during the pilot phase of the new system, when the CBA requirement had been suspended for obvious low-cost improvements. The problem took the IT department only a few minutes to correct. In its quest to build evidence for making the temporary suspension of CBA permanent for obvious small improvements, the design team went back and calculated that the delayed depositing of checks had been costing the company tens of thousands of dollars annually in lost interest.

Over the course of the pilot test, it became obvious that the company's emphasis on CBA had indeed imposed a huge barrier to many good ideas, and the policy mandating its use was permanently dropped except for ideas where larger expenditures were involved.

The second goal of the postpilot review is to determine what additional support-function resources will be needed once the idea system is launched organization-wide. As we discussed in Chapter 4, this information is difficult to gather in advance. But the experience gained from the pilot will provide a good indication of where more support-function resources will be needed.

The third goal of a postpilot review is to identify ways to make the organization-wide launch go as smoothly as possible. For example, at the U.S. military base mentioned earlier in this chapter, a concern emerged from the short pilot that middle managers (some of whom were midranking officers) were not observing enough idea meetings and doing enough coaching of their supervisors. When the middle managers heard this, they requested help with what exactly they should be looking for when appraising a team, and how they should respond to what they saw. As a result, a list of specific things to look for was generated, along with corresponding coaching and advising tips.

STEP 8
Roll Out the System Organization-wide

The pace and nature of an idea system launch depend on the organization's size, structure, culture, resources, and leadership team's sense of urgency. If the unit is small, it may make sense to train everyone together, and launch the whole system at once. But even in medium-sized units, rolling the system out gradually has a number of advantages. The first involves resources. Each department will require support during its startup phase. Managers, supervisors, and employees will all need to be trained and coached. Few organizations have the resources to do this for everyone at once. Pacing the rollout to match the available resources also destresses the launch and allows support functions such as IT, maintenance, purchasing, and engineering to more gradually adjust to their added responsibilities to help with front-line ideas. Furthermore, a phased rollout gives higher-level managers more time to get involved in each area's launch.

The second advantage of a gradual rollout is that each departmental launch benefits from the experience gained by its predecessors. The growing number of managers with deep expertise can be particularly helpful when rolling out the system to departments with special challenges—which is one reason that it is a good idea to schedule such departments later in the rollout.

A final advantage to a rollout launch is that departments with more reluctant managers can be scheduled near the end. By that time, they should have witnessed the system's success across the organization and have heard from their colleagues how helpful front-line ideas have been to them in meeting their goals. The momentum of the system and its obvious benefits makes continued resistance foolish.

Training

For a successful launch, significant training is needed at every level. Managers need to understand the philosophy behind the new idea system, their own roles in it, and how front-line ideas can be used to help them to achieve their group's goals. While much of the conceptual knowledge needed can be delivered through prelaunch workshops, the actual idea management skills can only be honed through practice and coaching. And the best place to get this practice and do this coaching is when managers are working with their own teams on real ideas in their own areas.

Many leaders make the mistake of throwing their supervisors into their new roles with little or no training. In idea-driven organizations, a supervisor's job switches from making sure that the work gets done to making sure that the *way* the work gets done is constantly improving.

Supervisors need training, practice, and coaching to develop the skills and attitudes required for this new mindset and role.

In the beginning, front-line employees will need a short training module on how to participate in the idea management process, but this is only the beginning. Most of their training will be done on an ongoing basis, and it should be primarily aimed at making them able to identify problems that were previously invisible to them. This is the focus of the next chapter.

STEP 9
Continue to Improve the System

An idea system is not a "fire and forget" initiative. Even mature idea-driven organizations are continually finding ways to improve how they manage ideas. For example:

- Allianz Slovakia (which in 2009 won the award for most innovative "Operating Entity" in Allianz's global network of 120 insurance companies) extended its idea system in 2010 to include its two-hundred-plus *independent* agents around Slovakia. Now, if agents have ideas or wish to report problems, a single function key on their computer opens a window that allows them to do so.

- The Utah group of Autoliv, the automotive safety systems company, has long been among the most idea-driven companies in the world, consistently averaging more than fifty implemented ideas per person. Over the last few years, its managers have implemented a number of initiatives to put extra emphasis on high-leverage areas for ideas. One, for example, was to set up a "*Jidoka* Wall of Heroes." *Jidoka* is the lean concept of stopping work to address problems or defects as they occur. The smallest problem, if not caught and corrected early, can become extremely costly later. When a worker flags a problem that could eventually become much larger, his or her picture and an explanation of the importance of that employee's actions are posted on the Wall of Heroes.

- When Pyromation discovered that most of each team's ideas were being implemented by only one or two people, it redesigned its idea process to assure that no one could work on more than two ideas at a time, and everyone would be assigned at least one.

No matter how much care goes into the initial design of your idea system, it should be made clear to everyone that the system will need to constantly evolve and improve. A system that is designed for continuous improvement should itself be continually improving.

KEY POINTS

We recommend a process for implementing an idea system that has the following nine steps:

Step 1. Make sure the leadership understands that a high-performing idea is a long-term initiative to create a significant new strategic capability. Then the leaders will have the patience and perseverance to provide the long-term leadership needed and be able to deploy the system in a strategic manner.

Step 2. Form and train the team that will design and implement the system. The team should have the power, credibility, and knowledge to design a system that integrates well with how the organization already works, to address the potentially significant organizational issues that will arise, and to lead the launch organization-wide.

Step 3. Assess the organization from an idea management perspective to identify misalignments, potential implementation challenges, and any existing systems that can be built upon or that should be integrated with the idea system.

Step 4. Design the idea system. The better the idea system can be integrated into existing practices and procedures, and the fewer new practices and procedures are created especially for it, the more easily and quickly it will be accepted as a regular part of the way the company works, and the better it will perform.

Step 5. Start correcting misalignments. Before the launch, it is important to eliminate obvious misalignments so that front-line teams can implement most of their ideas without undue heroics.

Step 6. Conduct a pilot test. Without a good pilot, many problems that are easy to correct if caught early become disruptive and difficult to deal with when the system is broadly deployed.

Step 7. Assess the pilot results, make adjustments, and prepare for the launch.

Step 8. Roll out the system organization-wide. The pace and nature of an idea system launch depends on the organization's size, structure, culture, resources, and leadership team's sense of urgency. In most situations, it is better to roll the system out in a measured fashion.

Step 9. Continue to improve the system. An idea system is not a "fire and forget" initiative. Even mature idea-driven organizations are continually finding ways to improve how they manage ideas. A system that is designed for continuous improvement should itself be continually improving.

7

Ways to Get More and Better Ideas

WHEN AN IDEA SYSTEM is launched, rarely is there a shortage of ideas. Front-line employees are already aware of many problems and opportunities that they have never had an easy way to correct before. Here, for example, are some of the early ideas at Big Y Foods:

- **(Bakery)** *Customers often ask if we sell the garlic butter we use to make garlic bread. I suggest we sell it in eight-ounce containers.*
- **(Checkout)** *The "tender" key for totaling an order is very close to the "clear sale" key on the touch screen cash registers. We often hit the "clear sale" key by accident instead, and delete the last sale. Have the IT department place these two keys farther apart.*
- **(Produce)** *Currently, stores call a special number to leave a message on an answering machine to report over/short deliveries in produce to be corrected in the next day's delivery. Since no one ever physically answers this phone, why is the answering machine set to pick up after nine rings, making every store's personnel wait thirty seconds unnecessarily every day?*
- **(Deli Counter)** *Why does it take nine keystrokes to key in a slice of pizza in the deli section? Please fix.*

- **(Meat Section)** *Put a mirror above the partition between the service counter and the back room where we cut the meat so we don't have to put down our work every three minutes to come out and see if a customer is waiting.*
- **(Groceries)** *We currently sell tubes of flavored ice unfrozen, for people to take home and freeze for their children. In the summer, why not put some in the freezer for impulse buys?*

These are all good ideas that were quickly implemented. But notice how they are also commonsense responses to problems that have made employees' jobs harder or are straightforward responses to repeated customer requests. Such ideas usually get an idea process off to a good start. But once the obvious problems have been addressed, the rate at which ideas come in typically slows dramatically. The remedy is to provide ongoing training and education to help your front-line people continually generate new types of ideas. This chapter is a primer of easy-to-use "street-smart" techniques to keep ideas coming in.

PROBLEM FINDING

In its most basic form, creativity can be divided into two parts: *problem finding* and *problem solving*. Historically, most organizations have focused on problem solving. This is only natural, because most organizations struggle to keep up with the onslaught of obvious problems that pop up in the normal course of daily work. Why would they go looking for more? A huge industry has built up around problem solving, and many books, tools, and training programs are available for help in this area.

A good idea system significantly multiplies an organization's problem-solving capacity, so it burns through the obvious problems faster than they come in. To keep improving, it has to get better at *problem finding*. This effort has two components: (1) developing employees' problem-finding skills and (2) creating organizational mechanisms that bring more problems to the surface.

Problem finding is a matter of perspective. So a quick and easy way to enhance your employees' problem-finding abilities is to expose them to fresh *perspectives* on how the organization can be improved. These alternative perspectives will cause them to see problems and opportunities that they would not have seen otherwise. Two methods to do this are *idea activators* and *idea mining.*

Idea Activators

Idea activators are short training or educational modules that teach people new techniques or give them new perspectives on their work that will trigger more ideas. Depending on the nature of the information to be imparted, these modules can be anything from a ten-minute talk to a formal classroom training session of several hours. To see how idea activators work, let us look at how Subaru Indiana Automotive (SIA) used a series of carefully targeted activators to reach the very ambitious goal mentioned briefly in Chapter 3.

In 2002, Fuji Heavy Industries, SIA's Japanese corporate parent, gave it the goal of becoming "zero landfill" by 2006. SIA's leadership team knew that to reach this goal in a cost-effective manner, they had to involve their front-line associates. They were the ones who first handled materials (such as packaging, used solvent, and steel scrap) after they had served their intended purpose and become waste.

However, the leadership team also knew that simply asking associates for their "green" ideas would not be enough. Most people have a fairly limited understanding of how to reduce an organization's environmental impact. For example, everyone knows about recycling, but most recycling offers only limited environmental advantages and is generally not cost effective. So SIA set out to increase its people's ability to spot green improvement opportunities by using idea activators. These activators introduced them to simple concepts that the company thought would spark large numbers of small ideas to eliminate landfill waste.

The Three Rs. SIA began with a brief orientation session on the Three Rs: reduce, reuse, recycle. The Three Rs are the central components of what is often referred to as the "waste management hierarchy" (see Figure 7.1). Starting from the *bottom,* this hierarchy ranks the different kinds of environmental actions in increasing order of environmental benefit:

FIGURE 7.1 The waste management hierarchy

- *Burning* material for energy is better than sending it to a landfill.
- *Recycling* it is better than burning it.
- *Reusing* material is better than recycling it.
- *Reducing* the amount needed is better than reusing it.
- *Eliminating* the need for material is better than reducing it.

The Three Rs framework was a good initial idea activator for SIA's purpose, because it was easy to remember and got people to think of ideas beyond simple recycling. Employees were taught to try to move what was done with waste materials further up the hierarchy, because this produced both greater environmental benefits and more cost savings.

One set of ideas, for example, moved the packaging for engine components from recycling to reuse. These components came from a Japanese supplier in large shipping containers, packed tightly in specially contoured protective Styrofoam blocks. Formerly, as employees unpacked these parts, they would put large amounts of Styrofoam into recycling bins. Recycling Styrofoam is expensive, as its low density increases handling and shipping costs, and it requires more processing and energy than most other polymers. But after Three R training, an employee team began to wonder whether it wouldn't be feasible to reuse this packaging. Since the empty shipping containers were already being sent back to the supplier, why couldn't they be repacked with the used Styrofoam so it could be reused by the supplier for a future shipment?

After analyzing the feasibility and costs of this, the team discovered that the idea would actually be profitable, and it quickly led to other ideas to return packaging materials to that supplier for reuse. Eventually, some eighty different kinds of plastic caps, metal clips, cardboard spacers, and various other packing materials were being returned to Japan for an annual savings of more than $3 million. When the Styrofoam packaging material is considered no longer suitable for reuse, the Japanese supplier melts it down and reuses the polymer to make new packaging material.

Other ideas, some extremely simple, reduced the company's usage of materials. One, for example, was to have parts arrive in open-topped boxes. Since they were delivered on wrapped pallets anyway, the tops weren't needed. This idea not only saved cardboard but also meant workers no longer had to use box cutters to open the boxes—hence, a safety and productivity improvement as well.

Dumpster Diving. If nothing was to be thrown away, everything put into the dumpsters had to be eliminated—recycled, reused, or not generated in the first place. Even the dumpsters themselves had to go. To this end, SIA developed another activator called "dumpster diving." Dumpster-diving teams overturned the dumpsters in their areas, spilling their contents onto the floor where they were sifted and sorted by source and type. Then the teams came up with ideas to deal with each type of waste using the Three Rs.

The effectiveness of this tactic is illustrated in the case of the dumpster that was located near the robotic welders used to assemble the car bodies. The dive team quickly realized that the "dirt" in the dumpster was actually the remnants of sparks generated during the welding process. These sparks are small particles of welding slag, which includes copper oxide blown off the copper welding tips by the arcing of the high-amperage electric current used to fuse the steel together. If zero landfill were the goal, sending the floor sweepings to the landfill would no longer be an option. After some searching, SIA found a company in Spain that could process the slag to recover the copper.

While processing the welding slag kept it out of the landfill, it was expensive to ship it to Spain (and the shipping added to the company's carbon footprint). So SIA set out to *reduce* the amount of sparks created in the welding process. Because sparks are caused by arcing between the copper welding tips and the steel, the better the fit between the tip and the steel, the fewer the sparks that are generated. A new tip of the proper shape sparks very little. But with use, the hot copper welding tips soften and deform, degrading the fit and creating more sparks. Because it is expensive and disruptive to replace the copper tips as they start to deform, standard practice is to increase the amperage on the welder every two hours to assure a good weld. The extra power produces even more sparks and heat, creating more tip deformation, which requires even more amperage, and so on. Now, instead of turning up the electricity when the tips deform, a special device mounted on each welder quickly machines them back to the optimal shape. The result—fewer sparks, less electricity used, and a 73 percent reduction in the number of welding tips consumed.

Compressed Air. The largest consumers of electricity at SIA were the air compressors. Compressed air was used extensively throughout the facility in a wide range of manufacturing processes. To reduce its consumption, SIA developed an idea activator that showed employees the high environmental and financial cost of generating compressed air and provided them with a number of clever tips on how to identify opportunities to cut its usage. This information resulted in thousands of ideas throughout the facility to plug air leaks and to replace O-rings in leaking pneumatic equipment, to improve maintenance regimes on air-powered tools and air cylinders, and to install shut-off valves for areas that did not need compressed air all the time. Here are some of the more creative ideas:

- Turning the plantwide compressed air level down from ninety-two pounds per square inch (psi) to eighty-seven, because the last few psi require a disproportionate amount of energy to generate and were not necessary—especially with the better-maintained pneumatic equipment

- Using a sensitive sound meter (when the facility is not operating and quiet) attached to a pole to listen to compressed air pipe joints high up near the ceiling for even tiny air leaks that humans couldn't hear
- Connecting two areas of the plant that had separate compressed air systems with an air pipe so that when combined demand was low enough, the two areas could share a single set of compressors

Cumulatively, the resulting front-line ideas to save compressed air cut the amount of electricity needed to generate compressed air in half, and SIA was able to take two of its four large air compressors offline.

Recycling Versus Downcycling. Another idea activator taught the difference between *recycling* and *downcycling.* Downcycling occurs when the method of recycling reduces the value or quality of the material. In most plastic recycling, for example, a wide assortment of different types and colors of plastics is melted down into an amorphous polymer blend useful only for low-value applications such as parking bumpers and plastic boards. Most "recycling" is actually downcycling. Whereas downcycling degrades the material, true recycling maintains its original physical characteristics and quality.

Armed with this new understanding, employees generated hundreds of ideas to change processes in order to avoid downcycling whenever possible. For example, a large number of ideas involved getting suppliers of different parts to use uncolored plastic of a standardized grade for packaging, so the different parts could be recycled together without degrading the value of the polymer.

SIA's green idea activators enabled its front-line employees to come up with large numbers of ideas without the need for disruptive and expensive formal training programs. Most of the activators were short enough to be delivered to work teams at their regular stand-up preshift team meetings. In the end, SIA sent its last waste shipment to a landfill in May 2004, two years ahead of its deadline, having also reduced its annual operating costs by millions of dollars.

Like at SIA, the specific sequence of idea activator training sessions that you need to develop will depend on your organization and its strategic goals. Some of these activators may be generic improvement tools that are already widely used to identify and solve common problems. By way of example, many lean tools—such as 5S (good housekeeping), *poka-yoke* (error-proofing), process charting, and value stream mapping—are reliable triggers for a large number of ideas. For instance, Bumrungrad Hospital in Bangkok, Thailand, one of the leading hospitals in the world, has radically reduced or almost entirely eliminated many kinds of medical errors through extensive application of *poka-yoke* principles at every stage of the health care delivery value stream.

Idea activators do not have to address only the major goals of top management. They can address smaller targets of opportunity as they are identified at the front-line level. For example, in a U.K. financial services company, many ideas requested the IT department to write Excel macros to save office workers' time on repetitive tasks. After seeing a number of these ideas over a few months, a middle manager suggested providing a quick idea activator on how to create Excel macros, so staff members could do it themselves. This certainly saved the IT function time, but it also triggered many ideas from people who could now see more applications for macros and also easily create them themselves.

Idea Mining

Many ideas have novel perspectives embedded in them. These perspectives are usually implicit, but if drawn out, they have the potential to trigger more ideas. The process of digging out these implicit novel perspectives is what we call *idea mining*.

We once witnessed a senior manager at a European insurance company put the concept to use immediately after a short training session on idea mining. Sitting in the back of an idea meeting in one of the company's small animal pet insurance call centers, we were observing the employees discuss problems and brainstorm ideas. One problem on their board was that customers were frequently calling the department for help with equine policies. The equine insurance division was in a different part of the country, and there was no way for the representatives to transfer these calls. Such calls were occurring some ninety times per week, and each wrong number took two or three minutes to deal with. The representative had to apologize, explain to the customer that he or she had called a wrong number and that there was no way the call could be transferred, wait for the customer to get a pencil and a notepad, provide the customer with the correct number, and perform any other needed service recovery. Two minutes per call, ninety times per week, meant that the problem was wasting about three hours per week.

One employee pointed out that the reason for all the wrong numbers was that the company's Yellow Page ad was confusing. The ad contained many phone numbers, and its graphics and layout made it easy for customers to call the wrong number. "I'll let the marketing department know, as they are about to place the new ads in this year's Yellow Pages," their manager said, and then began to move onto the next idea.

"Wait!" the senior manager piped up from the back. "Before you move on, let's make a new rule. *Every* time a customer is confused, let's write down the source of confusion on the idea board and see if we can fix the problem. When customers are confused, it is frustrating for them and wastes both their time and ours." He had noticed that the idea embodied a fresh perspective that the group could use to come up with new types of ideas to improve customer service. By drawing this new perspective out and making customer confusion a "problem flag" for the group, the senior manager made this single idea the seed of many more.

Not long afterward, we shared this example in a training session at a U.S. health insurance company. On our next visit, the idea system manager proudly remarked that the company had created its own problem flag. "Every time a customer calls, write down the reason why. After all, customers do not call just to say hello or to wish us Merry Christmas. They call because something we did, or did not do, made it necessary for them to call." Think of all the customer service improvements and other ideas that insight led to!

In our seminars, we often use an idea mining exercise to illustrate how easy it is to draw out novel perspectives from a set of ideas. For our explanation of this exercise, we will work with the sheet of "Ideas from the

Clarion-Stockholm Bar" given in Table 1.1. For convenience, we reproduce a numbered version of the sheet here as Table 7.1.

We begin by dividing the participants into small groups and asking each group to pick a number between one and eighteen (the number of ideas on the Clarion sheet). We then give them the idea sheet. Each group is asked to find the idea on the sheet that matches the number it picked. (Making participants pick their numbers *before* giving them the sheet keeps them from "cherry-picking" ideas to work with.)

We then instruct the groups to discuss their chosen ideas and consider the following questions, in order to identify any related ideas and tease out any novel perspectives that are implicit in their chosen idea:

- What other ideas does this one suggest?
- What other areas for improvement does this idea suggest?
- What fresh perspectives about how the organization can be improved does this idea suggest?

To show how this works, let us take the example of a group that picked the number six, which corresponds to Tim's idea:

Whenever the bar introduces a new cocktail, have a tasting for the restaurant staff, just as the restaurant always does when a new menu or menu item is introduced, so servers know what they are selling.

Here are some responses the group might have given for this particular idea:

- *Whenever the hotel introduces a new product or service, have the staff sample it and have it explained to them so they will be able to answer customer questions about it, will think of recommending it when appropriate, and be better able to sell it when they do.*
- *What other products and services could be sold more effectively if the staff were given the proper training and information about them?*
- *This is an example of improving cross-selling. One area (the restaurant) is selling products from another (the bar). In what other ways can we cross-sell products and services within the hotel?*

Although it is impractical to try to mine every idea, and not every idea is worth mining, it is astonishing how many potential perspectives can be

TABLE 7.1   Clarion Hotel Stockholm: Ideas from the bar

1.	*Marco*	Get maintenance to drill three holes in the floor behind the bar and install pipes so bartenders can drop bottles directly into the recycling bins in the basement.
2.	*Reza*	When things are slow in the bar, mix drinks at the tables so the guests get a show.
3.	*Nadia*	Many customers ask if we serve afternoon tea. Currently, there is no hotel in the entire south of Stockholm that does. I suggest we start doing this.
4.	*Tess*	Have an organic cocktail. Customers often ask for them, and we don't offer one.
5.	*Nadia*	Clarion conference and event sales staff often meet prospective customers in the bar. Give the bar staff information in advance about the prospects so they can be on alert and do something special.
6.	*Tim*	Whenever the bar introduces a new cocktail, have a tasting for the restaurant staff, just as the restaurant always does when a new menu or menu item is introduced, so servers know what they are selling.
7.	*Fredrik*	When the bar opens at 9:30 in the morning, many guests ask for vitamin shots (special blends of fruit juices). Put these on the menu.
8.	*Nadia*	Have maintenance build some shelves in an unused area in the staff access corridor behind the bar for glasses. Currently, there is so little space for glasses in the bar that they are stored upstairs in the kitchen, and it takes 30 minutes, several times a night, for one of the two bartenders to go and get glasses, which means lost sales.
9.	*Marco*	In the upstairs bar, we have to spend an hour bringing up all the alcohol from downstairs when we open and putting it away when we close. We wouldn't have to do this if locks were installed on the cabinets in the bar.
10.	*Marin*	On our receipts, when guests pay with Eurocard, it says "Euro." This confuses many guests, who think they have been charged in euros instead of kronor. Get the accounting department to contact our Eurocard provider to see if we can change the header on the receipts.
11.	*Nadia*	The bartending staff often act as concierges, telling people about the hotel, local shops, restaurants, and attractions, and giving directions. We have a concierge video that we show on our website. Offer this on the TVs in all hotel rooms.
12.	*Tess*	Currently we close at 10 p.m. on Sundays, and many guests complain about this. Because we have a red dot on our liquor license from a single violation many years ago, we must have four security guards in the bar to be open after 10 on Sundays, and this is too expensive. Apply to have red dot removed, and then we can stay open with only one security guard.

(continued)

TABLE 7.1 *(continued)* Clarion Hotel Stockholm: Ideas from the bar

13.	*Nadia*	The late night security guards are sometimes curt and rude to the customers (the security service is subcontracted). These guards should be required to take the same "Attitude at Clarion" training that all Clarion staff take.
14.	*Marco*	Increase the font size and make clearer that the coupons that conferences give out are for *discounts* at the bar, not for *free drinks.*
15.	*Nadia*	Have the kitchen mark the prewrapped ham sandwiches that the bar sells. Bar staff currently have to cut them in half to tell the difference between them and the ham-and-cheese sandwiches.
16.	*Marin*	Put an extra beer tap in the bar, so we can sell more beer. Currently, there is only one, and it is a bottleneck.
17.	*Nadia*	Have maintenance put some sandpaper safety strips on the handicapped ramp in the bar. Children currently use it as a slide, and the bar staff has to deal with minor scrapes and cuts on a daily basis.
18.	*Nadia*	Give the bar staff information about how many guests are staying in the hotel, so they can stock and staff the bar appropriately.

extracted from a routine set of ideas. Table 7.2 gives sample responses for just the first five ideas on the Clarion-Stockholm sheet. Moreover, the concept of idea-mining is not difficult to grasp and can easily be demonstrated and taught during a team's regular idea meeting.

The exercise just described is often eye-opening for managers. It shows them the value of targeted idea training and lays to rest the fear that sooner or later employees will run out of ideas. In fact, in our experience, rather than worrying about running out of ideas, after this exercise many managers become more concerned about being overwhelmed by them.

We recommend keeping track of some of the more useful perspectives that come out of idea mining in your meetings. Over time, you can build up a very useful list of broadly applicable questions that can be shared across your organization and used in problem-finding training and in training for new employees. Consider these examples:

TABLE 7.2 Perspectives drawn out of Clarion bar ideas

1. Get maintenance to drill three holes in the floor behind the bar and install pipes so bartenders can drop bottles directly into the recycling bins in the basement:
   - *What other things do bartenders have to leave the bar to fetch or do that could be streamlined or improved?*
   - *What aspects of the bartenders' jobs that are non-value-adding—i.e., that take them away from serving customers—can we eliminate or streamline?*
   - *Are there other places in the hotel where we can make recycling easier?*
   - *Can we reduce the amount of bottles and cans we use in the first place?*

2. When things are slow in the bar, mix drinks at the tables so the guests get a show:
   - *What other things can we do to make our service flashy and entertaining?*
   - *What other things could we do at the tables that would be different and interesting?*
   - *In what other ways could we use extra bartending capacity when things get slow?*

3. Many customers ask if we serve afternoon tea. Currently, there is no hotel in the entire south of Stockholm that does. I suggest we start one:
   - *What other drinks and foods are customers asking about, and can we provide these?*
   - *Afternoon tea is a British concept. What other national or ethnic traditions can we cater to?*
   - *What other things are offered in bars and hotels that we don't offer?*

4. Have an organic cocktail. Customers often ask for them, and we don't offer one.
   - *What other health needs or lifestyle trends (fair-trade, gluten-free, etc.) do our customers care about?*
   - *Are there any fashion/political trends we can offer drinks in line with?*
   - *Ask customers for ideas about drinks we currently don't offer that they would like.*

5. Clarion conference and event sales staff often meet prospective customers in the bar. Give the bar staff information in advance about the prospects so they can be on alert and do something special.
   - *What other potential customers are brought to the bar—birthday parties, weddings, and other events—that it would be useful for the bar staff to know about in advance?*
   - *What kinds of special services can bartenders provide, and which will work best?*
   - *What other visitors to the bar may be particularly important to the hotel—VIPs, famous people—and could the bar get a heads-up on those people too?*
   - *What other hotel services could bar staff be involved in selling?*
   - *Might there be ways to do "something special" for all guests?*

- Every time a customer asks you for something you or your organization can't do, ask why it isn't currently possible and what could be done to make it possible.
- Anytime it takes you more than fifteen seconds to find something, ask why.
- Anytime something comes back to you or your group because it was not done correctly the first time, ask why.
- Anytime customers ask questions or seem confused, ask why.
- Anytime you realize that you or your coworkers are making mistakes due to a poor process, think what could be changed.
- Anytime you throw something out, ask why it is there in the first place (a green perspective).

The Clarion-Stockholm Hotel also encourages its people to use two additional "digging" techniques that are similar in spirit to idea mining: *aggressive listening* and *thoughtful observation*. An example of aggressive listening is that when guests come to reception to check out, the staff will always ask them how their stay was. If a guest has a complaint, the front-desk clerk is careful to get all the details he or she can in order to fully understand what happened. So far, this is no different from most good hotels. The difference comes when a guest responds with simply "Fine" or "OK," but the clerk can tell that something might be bothersome. The staffer will not simply let it go at that and will politely probe further. When such deeper inquiry is done properly, it becomes a pleasant and sincere conversation while the guest's receipt is being processed. The guest is sharing a concern or observation with a "friend" that they would normally not mention to a stranger. Think of how many times you have wanted to tell a hotel checkout person about a problem or give a suggestion about how the hotel could do better, but held back because you felt the staffer was not really interested.

The Clarion-Stockholm also encourages its employees to observe customers closely to notice subtler problems and opportunities that customers may not formally articulate. One astute observation, for example, came from a server in the dining room. She noticed that many customers left their reading glasses at home and had trouble reading the menu. Her suggestion: have a box with various strengths of reading glasses to lend to diners who need them.

The increased thoughtfulness about the guest experience results in some unique touches at the hotel. For example, one day a guest arrived in a panic. He was about to lead a workshop, the battery on his laptop computer was almost dead, and he had forgotten to bring his charger. A member of the front desk staff scoured the hotel to find one that would work. Once the guest's problem was solved, the staffer submitted an idea: purchase spare chargers for the most popular laptop computers for guests with emergencies, and keep these chargers on hand in the hotel's two business centers.

CREATING A PROBLEM-SENSITIVE ORGANIZATION

Our focus so far in this chapter has been on ways to enhance *individual* problem sensitivity. This section looks at how to use policies and processes to increase an *organization's* problem sensitivity.

Graniterock is a Malcolm Baldrige National Quality Award–winning supplier of rock, sand, gravel, concrete, asphalt, and other materials to the construction industry south of San Francisco, California. In 1989, CEO Bruce Woolpert introduced his "short-pay" policy, which states that "If you [the customer] are not satisfied, . . . don't pay us." If a customer is not satisfied with some aspect of the products or services he receives from Graniterock, he simply deletes the relevant charge on its invoice and pays the rest.

According to Woolpert, organizations are very skilled at building thick "defensive crusts" that isolate them from customer complaints. The short-pay policy was put in place to cut through this crust by making sure that customers voiced their problems and that the organization acted on them.

Before putting the policy in place, Woolpert made sure his organization was ready for it. As he put it to us:

When we introduced the short-pay policy, I was very careful to go around and make sure that people felt—in their hearts and in their minds—that we really should not be paid if we didn't make someone happy. The reason I did this was that I wasn't sure what the reaction would be to a customer actually doing a short-pay . . . because it could seem that doing a short-pay is a confrontational thing, but it's not. . . . We made sure people felt that it was really unethical to make people pay for something for which they really didn't receive good value.

Once the policy was introduced, the company promoted it heavily; and in the first year some six hundred short-pays cost the company the equivalent of 2.3 percent of its sales. While this would be a major sacrifice for any company, it was even more so for Graniterock, because the gravel and concrete industry operates on particularly low margins. Today, with a lot of problem solving under its belt, the cost of Graniterock's short-pay policy is under 0.2 percent of sales, far less than what most companies set aside for returns.

When a customer short-pays, Graniterock goes through a process to understand the incident and fix the problem. The customer is called immediately, given an apology, and assured that the short-pay has already been taken off the bill and that the purpose of the call is for Graniterock to learn and improve. Once the customer understands that the call is not about the money, he or she is asked to explain the incident in detail so the Graniterock team can understand exactly why he or she was disappointed. Here are several examples of improvements the short-pay policy has triggered:

- The biggest problem the short-pay system flagged early on was poor on-time delivery performance. Part of the reason was that the company didn't have a good dispatching system—the dispatching office used large poster-sized sheets of paper on the wall to write down orders as they came in, and highlighter pens to track the status of the loads throughout the day. On busy days, it was hard for dispatchers to keep track of all of the information coming in, and deliveries would inevitably fall behind. The improvement team searched for software that could help. Today, there are plenty of options, but back in 1989 the company had to create its own dispatching software by adapting software designed for other industries.

- Another recurring reason for early short-pays (more than fifty in the first year) was problems with colored concrete. Customers would order concrete in different colors, usually red, beige, or some other earth tone. Many contractors short-paid because the color of the concrete was too light or it was blotchy. In these situations, Graniterock was not only hit by the short-pay itself but also often paid for the concrete to be torn up and replaced. At the time, poor color control was the norm in the concrete industry. Every concrete vendor had problems with color consistency, and Graniterock was no different. But for the contractors who had to put up with it, it was a huge problem. Colored concrete is typically used in highly visible places as part of the design concept, such as elaborate patios or swimming pool areas. Although Graniterock had known of the problem, it was only when its teams began visiting the short-paying customer sites that it realized how big the problem actually was. Before the short-pay policy, Graniterock had received only a few complaints about color each year and had never considered the problem to be significant.

  Standard industry practice was to add color after the concrete had been loaded in the delivery mixer trucks. The driver would climb up on a loading platform, cut open the heavy bags of coloring powder, and pour the powder into the concrete. The powder then mixed into the concrete on the way to the customer's site. Before short-pay, when the company had gotten complaints, it had assumed the problem was a dosage error, and someone from the main office would contact the driver to ask how many bags he had put in. Often, the driver couldn't remember and was simply reminded to be more careful next time. Now that the short-pay policy was making the problem expensive, the Graniterock team began trying to find its root cause in earnest. It turned out that the problem wasn't the dosages, but *clumping*. Even when the driver added the correct amount, the dry powder would often clump as it entered the wet concrete and not get blended in thoroughly. So Graniterock found suppliers who could provide the color in liquid form, and the problem was solved.
- Another recurring short-pay problem arose from late deliveries to construction sites in new areas whose roads were not yet on the maps.

Drivers often spent significant amounts of time driving around look-ing for the sites. The solution was to use fire department maps, which by regulation had to have all information up-to-date. A collage of fire department maps was put up on a large wall in the dispatching area so drivers could study it and visualize where their construction sites were.

- Individual short-pays alerted Graniterock to the fact that customers often had unique unstated needs that they simply assumed the com-pany would meet. For example, some customers would state a deliv-ery time but expect the truck to actually arrive fifteen minutes before the concrete was to be poured. Others would expect certain quality and performance additives in every load. These were an added cost, so Graniterock would not include them unless they were specified in the order. But some customers expected these mixes in every load, whether stated or not. After looking into the reasons behind these kinds of short-pays, it turned out that as Graniterock was improving its service, its regular customers were increasingly looking upon it as a partner, and they expected the company to remember their particular requirements. As Woolpert put it, "the short-pay system taught us over time how unique two-thirds of our customers are."

In the beginning of the drive to improve delivery times, Woolpert had made a bet with a friend—the owner of the regional franchise for Domi-no's Pizza, a company renowned for its on-time delivery. The bet was about which company would have the better delivery performance over a speci-fied period. The losing company would supply the winner with pizza for all its employees. In the end, Graniterock won in some cities, Domino's in others, and the bet was declared a wash.

After more than twenty years of operating with short-pay, the company has fixed its more obvious customer-related problems. Today, its short-pay system continues to dig deeper and identify subtler and subtler issues for Graniterock to tackle, giving the company capabilities that its competitors lack. In recent years, the company has developed such a strong reputation for quality that inspectors sometimes waive tests when they find out that Graniterock delivered the concrete. They know the concrete has already passed more stringent tests at Graniterock than they would put it through.

And many of its customers told us that they were willing to pay a premium to buy from Graniterock, because there would be fewer headaches, and the ease of doing business with the company meant that their total costs for many jobs would actually be lower. The company is also a leader in making "green concrete"—that is, concrete that is more environmentally friendly without sacrificing any loss in its engineering performance.

Organizational problem sensitivity requires an infrastructure that makes it easy to capture, analyze, and solve problems. The Clarion-Stockholm puts terminals in behind-the-scenes corridors and staff areas to make it easy for employees to record problems. The application used is the same one that is used to capture ideas, and it categorizes customer problems in a way that makes them easy to analyze. Among other things, this approach allows the hotel to build a stronger case for headquarters in Norway when a bigger problem needs corporate-level involvement or resources. For example, when the hotel first installed Internet in the rooms, the system—which had been negotiated centrally for all hotels by headquarters with the Internet provider—required customers to use cards with access codes that were valid for only eight hours. Guests were supposed to drop by the front desk each day to get their free card and to buy any additional cards if needed. From the outset, customers complained about this system. If a business guest checked e-mail in the morning for ten minutes, the access code would have expired by the time that guest returned at the end of the day.

The receptionists had been telling their supervisors about the guest discontent from the beginning, the supervisors had been telling hotel management, and management had tried to persuade headquarters to negotiate a less cumbersome arrangement with the Internet provider—all to no avail. However, after the idea system was put in place, the staff was able to document the high volume of guest complaints on this topic and demonstrate the extent of the problem. Headquarters relented and renegotiated a better contract.

A similar situation arose with the ventilation system. From the moment the hotel opened, the guests complained incessantly about it. Certain floors had little air circulation and were often stuffy. Unfortunately, it would require a major capital project costing several million dollars to correct the problem, and headquarters was reluctant to authorize the expense. But after being confronted with reports of hundreds of guest complaints about poor ventilation, headquarters got the message and contracted to have the problem corrected.

KEY POINTS

✓ When an idea system is launched, rarely is there a shortage of ideas. Front-line employees are already aware of many problems and opportunities that they have never had a way to correct before. But once the obvious problems have been addressed, the rate at which ideas come in typically slows dramatically. The remedy is ongoing training and education to continually sensitize front-line people to new types of problems.

✓ Creativity can be divided into *problem finding* and *problem solving*. Historically, most organizations have focused on problem solving. But a good idea system significantly multiplies an organization's problem-solving capacity, so it will burn through the obvious problems faster than they come in. To keep improving, an organization has to get better at *problem finding*.

✓ Problem finding is often a matter of perspective. An easy way to enhance your employees' problem-finding abilities is to expose them to fresh perspectives on how the organization might be improved. This will help them to see problems and opportunities that they would not have seen otherwise.

✓ *Idea activators* are short training or educational modules that teach people new techniques or give them new perspectives that will trigger more ideas.

✓ Many ideas have novel perspectives embedded in them. These perspectives are usually implicit, but if drawn out, they have the potential to trigger more ideas. The process of digging out these implicit novel perspectives is called *idea mining*.

✓ Graniterock's "short-pay" policy—"if you the customer are not satisfied, . . . don't pay us"—is an example of a system to increase an *organization's* problem sensitivity.

8

Front-Line Ideas and Innovation

ALL OVER THE WORLD, leaders are struggling with the question of how to make their organizations more innovative. For the majority of them, their first step should be to set up a high-performing idea system. This approach will allow them to take advantage of the powerful multi-faceted synergies between front-line ideas and innovations. Without these synergies in play, their organizations are far less innovative than they could be.

In this chapter, we explain why the ability to get large numbers of bottom-up ideas significantly increases an organization's ability to produce breakthrough innovations on a consistent basis. First, the synergies between front-line ideas and innovations lead to more and bigger breakthroughs. Second, putting a high-performance idea system in place requires the organization to be realigned, which eliminates many of the same barriers that also make the innovation process so difficult—barriers that would otherwise be ignored.

INNOVATIONS OFTEN NEED
FRONT-LINE IDEAS TO WORK

The complexity and novelty of large innovations mean that many smaller ideas are required to get them to work effectively, or sometimes even to work at all. To see this, let us look at a major green innovation that took place at Subaru Indiana Automotive (SIA) during its drive to zero landfill discussed in the last chapter.

One of the more toxic chemicals in the automobile manufacturing industry is the solvent used to flush paint systems between color changes. At SIA, this typically occurs every three or four vehicles. Previously, the toxic used solvent was shipped off-site for processing, a costly affair that required special handling and transportation procedures. An employee had the idea to develop an on-site distillation process to recover the solvent for reuse. When looking for vendors of such technology, SIA found one that proposed an innovative approach that would be significantly more environmentally friendly. Traditional distillation technology left a highly toxic sludge of paint residue and solvent in the bottom of the still. This vendor suggested a new approach: distill the solvent in a vacuum. Vacuum distillation would make it possible to extract almost all of the toxic solvent and leave only a trace in a dry cake in the bottom of the still. SIA liked the idea and gave the vendor the contract.

Unfortunately, the vendor struggled to get the new technology to work, and it went bankrupt before succeeding. The responsibility for completing the project fell onto the shoulders of one of SIA's maintenance crews. By the end of the project, these workers had come up with hundreds of small ideas that cumulatively solved the problems that the vendor's engineers could not. With the new vacuum distillation process in place—the first of its kind in the industry—the company's solvent use dropped from three to five truckloads a month to less than one every quarter, and the need to truck tankerloads of contaminated solvent off-site for processing was eliminated.

Additional front-line ideas quickly exploited the innovation and enhanced its impact. Rather than shipping the dry still-bottom residue to a special toxic-waste incineration plant almost five hundred miles away, an employee suggested a way to recycle it. She identified a company that could extract the organic elements from the still-bottom residue and reuse them. The char left over from this organic recovery process went to local steel companies that used it in the protective coatings they applied to the ladles they used to pour molten steel.

Another idea involved the rags used to clean the painting equipment. As had been the case with the solvent-contaminated sludge, solvent-soaked rags needed to be shipped as toxic waste to the special incineration plant. A worker suggested that the rags could be centrifuged to extract the solvent, which could then be distilled for reuse. The idea worked. For every thirty-four barrels of rags that were centrifuged, one barrel of solvent was recovered. This, in turn, led to another idea. Since the polyester rags no longer held toxic solvent, they could now be recycled. They were sold to a company that used them as raw materials in making the plastic for the wheel-well linings it manufactured for another auto company. So, ironically, one of Subaru's waste streams ended up in a competitor's cars.

Suppose Subaru had been unable to tap the front-line ideas it needed to get the distillation process working. Instead of pioneering an innovative green solvent recovery system and building on it to eliminate other streams of waste, it would have been hauling away a bunch of useless new distillation equipment, and returning to a more expensive, much more environmentally damaging approach to handling solvents.

FRONT-LINE IDEAS CREATE CAPABILITIES THAT ENABLE INNOVATIONS

Large numbers of small ideas can create substantial new strategic capabilities that allow an organization to innovate in ways that would otherwise be impossible. In 2009, Allianz China won an award from one of China's leading financial newspapers for that year's "Most Innovative Life Insurance Product." Called "Super Fit," the product was a totally customizable life insurance policy, for which customers could choose their benefit and payment periods, select from a menu of "rider" options for various causes of death, and tailor the maturity payouts to their personal needs. The idea for the product came from a staffer who had been talking with a friend who had just purchased life insurance. The friend was thirty-one years old and, due to his financial situation, had wanted to pay premiums over eleven years, with the amounts based on his lucky numbers. But no insurance company offered that kind of flexibility in how life insurance policies were structured. The staffer wanted to know whether there was some way for Allianz China to offer customers the ability to tailor their policies to their needs, whatever these were. Focus groups loved the idea, and the company began developing a flexible life insurance product.

As we discussed in Chapters 2 and 3, when CEO Wilf Blackburn took over Allianz China, one of his first actions had been to start an idea system. The ideas this system brought in, he told us, had over time made the company extraordinarily flexible, which is what enabled it to both create and deliver such an innovative product. Unique products are rare in the Chinese insurance market, because competitors copy each other's new products within months. But *two years* after Super Fit was launched, senior managers at a leading competitor were still expressing amazement at how Allianz China could offer such a flexible product.

FRONT-LINE IDEAS CAN TRANSFORM ROUTINE INNOVATIONS INTO MAJOR BREAKTHROUGHS

Some years ago, Task Force Tips (TFT), the innovative firefighting equipment maker discussed in Chapter 3, came up with an interesting new product idea at a firefighting equipment trade show. During the show, several distributors stopped by its display booth and asked when TFT was going to add a "monitor" to its product line. A monitor is a large water cannon that is fed by several fire hoses and is used to spray large quantities of water onto major fires from safe distances. This was not the first time that customers had asked about a monitor, and the company was well aware of this gap in its product line. But TFT had a long-standing policy that it would develop a new product only if it would be clearly superior to every other similar product on the market, and the company had not yet figured out how to do this with a monitor.

The problem with monitors was that, while they were very effective at fighting larger fires, they were also heavy (typically requiring two fire-fighters to carry and set up) and dangerous to operate. The pressure of the water coming from several hoses meant that extra care had to be taken when setting up the monitor and anchoring it to the ground. Even when the monitor was properly anchored, a pressure surge in the water mains could tear the monitor loose and cause it to buck up and lash around like an angry snake. Many firefighters have been injured or killed by out-of-control monitors.

One evening during the trade show, the TFT team met to review that day's activities. The group got to talking about the latest round of requests for TFT to develop a monitor. Some team members felt strongly that the company should do it, others—including Stuart McMillan, the presi-dent—felt strongly that it should not. A lively discussion ensued. McMillan reiterated the company policy of making only products that were clearly superior to those of its competitors, and he observed that there was no way to correct the basic problems with monitors.

The vice president for sales disagreed, "All we need to do is to add a pressure gauge so firefighters can see when a pressure surge is happening."

McMillan's immediate response was "How is a firefighter supposed to watch a gauge while fighting a fire? Even if he could, the gauge would report the problem only after it happened—too late for the firefighter to shut off or get away from the bucking water cannon." As an aside, he commented, "It would be better if the monitor simply shut off when it started bucking."

Everyone knew immediately that McMillan had stumbled onto a potential solution. A monitor that would automatically shut off when it lifted off the ground would be *much* safer.

Back at the company, McMillan scheduled a concept meeting to discuss how TFT might use the shut-off idea to create a superior monitor. Everyone interested in participating was invited to a pizza party and brainstorming session. More than twenty people came, including many front-line work-ers who were also volunteer firefighters. In addition to consuming a lot of pizza, the participants generated ideas for *twenty-one* unique features for the new TFT monitor, including spring steel legs (rather than cast iron) so that the monitor would automatically sit level on uneven ground and not need to be shimmied level; sharp tungsten carbide teeth at the end of each leg designed to bite into clay, asphalt, or even concrete in order to keep the monitor from shifting; a special electrodeposited coating that would never wear off like regular paint; laser-etched (rather than stenciled) instructions and safety warnings; a special design to shoot the water from a central point much closer to the ground in order to provide greater stability; lightweight aluminum cast construction; cranks for adjusting the direction of the nozzle both vertically and horizontally; tie-down straps stored inside the monitor and attached to one of the caps so that when firefighters pulled the cap off to attach the hose, the tie-down strips would pop out and they wouldn't forget to lash down the monitor; and, of course, a pressure gauge. In accordance with TFT's new product policy, the monitor was clearly superior to its competitors. It was less than half the weight, more versatile and compact, and easier to use. Most important, it was much, much safer than the other monitors on the market. The product ultimately received a patent and won an award for the best new product of the year from the International Association of Fire Chiefs. It was the first in a TFT line of innovative new monitors and water cannons.

While McMillan's idea to cut off the water when the monitor bucked had provided the starting point, it was the additional ideas from TFT's people that made the new product truly exceptional.

TFT has a number of ongoing ways to assure that front-line ideas are integrated into all its design work. For example, the design department has a door opening directly onto the manufacturing floor. When designing or modifying products, designers work closely with production workers to capture their ideas on how to improve the designs and make them more manufacturable. This close working relationship also allows machinists to keep the design staff up to speed on newly acquired manufacturing technologies and the added capabilities they provide.

As we mentioned earlier, many TFT employees already understand their customers' needs well because they are volunteer firefighters themselves. Even so, the company is always on the lookout for creative approaches to deepen its workers' appreciation of the needs of its customers. For example, a few years ago, when gasoline prices jumped during the summer driving season, McMillan overheard several employees talking about their summer vacation plans. One worker was saying that because of the high gasoline prices, he and his family were going to stay closer to home. McMillan learned that other employees were also cutting back on their vacation travel for the same reasons. He thought this situation was unfortunate, and it led him and his management team to come up with a creative way to help employees with their summer vacations while also helping to promote the company a bit. They launched the "Take Family Traveling" (yes, the "TFT") program. While on vacation anywhere in the continental United States, if the worker was willing to visit a fire station, he or she would be reimbursed twenty-five cents per mile for the round-trip distance (according to MapQuest) between that station and TFT and receive a modest additional sum (depending on the destination) to offset other expenses. (Naturally, the employees were careful to visit the fire stations at the farthest point of their journey away from TFT!) Workers were expected to introduce themselves and TFT to the firefighters, get their picture taken with them in front of the station, and give them a bag of paraphernalia, which included some innovative TFT safety gadgets and information about the company and its products. When the employees returned from vacation, the photos were posted on a bulletin board, and pins were placed on a nearby map to designate the locations of the fire stations visited.

TFT's active integration of front-line knowledge into its product development processes has given it a major advantage over its competitors. Even though it is still only a relatively small organization of 150 people, over the last two decades, the company has moved from being a minor player in the firefighting industry to a global provider of firefighting equipment recognized in the industry for its extraordinary innovativeness.

FRONT-LINE IDEAS CAN OPEN UP NEW OPPORTUNITIES FOR INNOVATION

In 2011 *Fast Company* magazine ranked Whirlpool Corporation sixth on its list of the world's most innovative consumer products companies. A decade earlier, the company would have never been considered for such a list.

In the late 1990s, Whirlpool CEO David Whitwam became concerned that the home appliances industry was rapidly becoming a commodity business. Prices for appliances were dropping and Whirlpool's margins were declining every year. As Whitwam put it at the time, when a customer walked into any large appliance store, he would be confronted with a "sea of white"—rows of white appliances with little difference between brands. The machines were all the same color, and all had the same basic features. With such little differentiation, whenever a washer or dryer needed to be replaced, customers would simply buy the single unit they needed with little thought to matching their brand to their current machine. As a result, in 2000 Whirlpool's average washer/dryer match rate was only 15 percent, and its average sale per customer purchase was $698.

Whitwam was convinced that Whirlpool had to become an innovator if it was to avoid a commodity trap, and he embarked on a mission to transform the company. He promoted Nancy Tennant Snyder to the position of vice president of core competencies and leadership development, charging her with "embedding innovation" into everything Whirlpool did. The company hired an outside consulting company to develop a broad range of new systems to promote innovation and new training programs designed to change the mental models of its managers. Transforming a large, sleepy midwestern manufacturer into an innovative global consumer products company was not easy and took more than a decade, but Whirlpool's global market share rose dramatically as a result.

New Whirlpool appliances were introduced to the market in many different colors and with new high-tech features that greatly enhanced performance. Customers could buy washers that used much less water and detergent, cleaned clothes better and extended clothing life, extracted more water in the spin cycles to make drying faster and more energy-efficient, and had a wide variety of cleaning cycles. New dryers could steam the wrinkles out of clothes and even dry-clean them. By 2006, Whirlpool had moved its washer/dryer match rate to an impressive 96 percent and had increased the average customer sale more than threefold, to $2,398.

In the old Whirlpool, all of the innovation came from R&D, engineering, or product development. But when the embedding effort reached the front lines, the workers, too, came up with some very innovative ideas. For example, one worker pointed out that most people put laundry, detergent, and other things on the tops of their washers and dryers. But when the machines run, they vibrate and these objects fall off, often slipping into tight spaces around and between the machines where they are difficult to recover. The worker's idea was for the company to sell custom-fitted rubber tops with lips around the edges for each of its machine pairs. A second new product idea came from a worker in the area that fabricated the platforms the company sold to elevate front-loading washers and dryers. Raising front-loading washers and dryers by twelve to fifteen inches reduces the need for as much bending and makes the machines more accessible. The worker's idea: incorporate drawers into these platforms to turn them into convenient storage spaces. These and other ideas have led to a line of ancillary products called Laundry 1-2-3, which includes storage cabinets that match the various appliance color options and fit snugly alongside the washer and dryer, laundry carts, adjustable clothing racks, and other products to organize the laundry room. The margins on these items are much higher than those for the appliances themselves, and they helped to increase the average customer sale to over $3,000.

SETTING UP AN IDEA SYSTEM REMOVES MANY OF THE BARRIERS TO INNOVATION

As we have discussed, most organizations are poorly aligned for ideas, whether these ideas are for modest improvements or breakthrough innovations. Consequently, innovations require a great deal of championing, in the form of managers exercising clout to override misalignments or using their guile, influence, and connections to circumvent them. All this effort is simply accepted as part of what is needed to innovate, so the underlying misalignments are rarely corrected. This means that the same high level of effort will be required for the next innovation, and every one after that. This huge hidden cost cuts deeply into an organization's innovative capacity without management ever realizing it.

But when an organization launches a high-performing idea system, those same misalignments rise up and smack management in the face. It is impossible to handle large numbers of bottom-up ideas with the "champions battling barriers" model. First, the ideas involved are generally small, and their individual impacts do not justify the effort required to fight the system to implement each one. Second, their sheer quantity would overwhelm any ad hoc approach relying on work-arounds. So when organizations set up high-performing idea systems, they are forced to identify and address where they are misaligned for ideas.

Consider how the implementation of an idea system at HCSS, a Houston-based developer of software for the construction industry, forced the company to deal with some major alignment issues. This fast-growing company had a lot going for it. It already provided the leading software for bidding on medium-to-large horizontal construction projects (i.e., roads and related infrastructure), was known for outstanding customer service (its Net Promoter Score [NPS] consistently averaged in the 80s range), had been recognized by the *Wall Street Journal* as a "Top Small Workplace," and had been named by Best Companies Group as "One of the Best Companies to Work for in Texas" for each of the previous six years. Despite HCSS's success, owner and president Michael Rydin was concerned that as it had grown rapidly to a 140-person company, it had lost some of its innovativeness. He thought that a high-performance idea system would reenergize his company.

The development team responsible for HeavyBid, the company's most popular software product, was chosen as a pilot area for the idea system. In the team's first discussion about the new system, a particularly troublesome blockage in the flow of ideas came up. Each of the company's software products was updated two or three times a year, and the new features, functions, and other improvements in these releases were critically important for retaining existing customers and attracting new ones. Departments that were in regular contact with customers—such as technical support, customer training, and product implementation—always had many ideas for improvements. In addition, top managers had changes they wanted to see based on strategic concerns and conversations with major customers, the sales department had ideas about features based on inquiries from current and potential customers, and the programmers themselves had their own ideas on how to improve each version. But the company could only focus on a limited number of enhancements for each release, and there was no clear process for capturing, evaluating, and prioritizing them.

When HCSS was smaller, people in the different roles talked regularly, and any differences in opinions about potential improvements were addressed informally. But with growth, work became increasingly segmented and departmentalized. Each department continued to refine its own procedures and processes in order to coordinate and improve its own work. Incrementally, barriers were raised between the departments, making it increasingly difficult for groups to work together informally.

The lack of clear processes to capture and prioritize product improvement ideas resulted in an ad hoc approach to determining which ones to move ahead with. Sometimes various middle managers would champion specific ideas, and sometimes top managers would step in to "encourage" consideration of their ideas. But the primary responsibility for selecting what to include fell to the programming teams and their managers. This led to a lot of problems. When a new version was demonstrated internally before its release, the various constituencies typically insisted on a great many "corrections," and often top management would add some critical new feature at the last minute or catch one that somehow had been left out. The result was a great deal of rework, delays, and tension between the programming teams and other groups in the company. Before any real traction could be expected with the idea system in the pilot area, this problem had to be addressed.

Consequently, much of the early work of the pilot team went into developing effective processes for capturing and prioritizing product improvement ideas. The process included regimes to (1) capture product improvement ideas from the various areas of the company, (2) estimate the programming time that each would take, (3) project the impact of each idea, (4) prioritize the list of ideas, and (5) select which were to be included in the new release. Furthermore, great care went into how and when changes that were identified once the development cycle had started would be considered for incorporation into the new release.

The impact of the new process to capture product improvement ideas was apparent in the very next development cycle. Technical support staff and other high-customer-contact teams reported that many more of their ideas—both big and small—were considered and included. Because top managers were engaged earlier in the process, they added fewer of their ideas late in the development process, when they would be more disruptive and cause significant delays. In short, the new process allowed more and better ideas to be included in new releases.

While many people in HCSS knew there were problems in how the company identified what went into new releases, it was only when HCSS chose to implement a high-performing idea system that the issue could no longer be avoided. Removing this misalignment led directly to some major innovations.

For example, the lack of a process to prioritize changes was so disruptive to the HeavyBid development team's work processes that they had difficulty thinking about how to improve them. Once the new process to capture product improvement ideas was in place, however, the team could think seriously about how its own processes worked. During an idea meeting, a part-time programmer proposed a novel idea for how to automate the testing of the team's programming work. If the idea worked, it would cut more than two weeks and hundreds of hours out of each development cycle. HeavyBid was highly complex software with many interrelated features and functions that had been built, modified, and added to by many programmers over several decades. Sometimes, even a minor "improvement" in one module created new problems elsewhere in the software. Previously, the full testing to find these problems was done at the end of the development cycle, taking several weeks or more to ensure the elimination of all critical bugs. The idea made it possible to develop software that could automatically test the impact of modifications on a daily basis. The testing routine would run overnight to check the effect of any changes made during the day, and problems could then be quickly identified and fixed.

Although automated testing of software was hardly new, a number of unique aspects of the HeavyBid product and its structure meant that the amount of skilled programming time that it would normally take to develop an automated testing regime would be astronomical. What the part-time programmer suggested was a highly creative way to relatively quickly develop an automated testing program that could check HeavyBid's more than a hundred thousand lines of code. Her idea was improved upon by several other programmers on her team, and with the help of several summer interns, the project was completed with only a few hundred hours of regular HCSS employee time. This was less time than the new testing regime would save in every development cycle from then on.

BRINGING IT ALL TOGETHER

To this point, we have been discussing how front-line ideas help individual aspects of innovativeness. But because the interplay between front-line ideas and innovation takes place on so many different dimensions and levels at the same time, it cannot really be understood without stepping back and taking a holistic view.

A good example of how being idea driven enables an organization to innovate across the board is illustrated by ThedaCare, a Wisconsin-based, not-for-profit health care organization with some six thousand employees in its network of hospitals, primary care and specialty clinics, and facilities for assisted living, long-term care, and hospice.

In many ways, the medical field has been a model of innovation. Technological breakthroughs allow doctors today to treat conditions that were once considered to be life-threatening as routine outpatient procedures and to address problems that would have been beyond their capabilities just a few years ago. But while the U.S. health care system may have some of the best technology in the world, overall it is costly and inefficient, and delivers poor clinical results. Soon, the United States will be spending some 20 percent of its gross domestic product (GDP) on health care, far more than any other country, yet the quality of health care was ranked thirty-seventh by the World Health Organization, below countries such as Costa Rica and Colombia.[1] Approximately one hundred thousand people die each year in the United States due to medical errors. According to Dr. Lucian Leape, a noted patient safety expert, people would have to ride in motorized hang gliders or parachute off bridges to face similar risks to being a patient in a U.S. hospital.[2] This poor performance has resulted from a stark lack of innovation, not in the technology available, but in the *way health care is delivered*. The delivery process is exactly where Theda-Care focused its innovation efforts.

ThedaCare began experimenting with the application of lean principles in 2002. At the time, the organization was already recognized for its clinical results. In both 2000 and 2001, it had received the highest scores in the United States on the Health Employers Data Information Sets (HEDIS)—a body of quality-of-care measures used by the National Committee for Quality Assurance, the U.S. accrediting body for health plans. But John Toussaint, ThedaCare's CEO at the time, believed that the organization could—and *had* to—do much better. Too many avoidable mistakes were being made that could cause harm to patients. Prior to becoming CEO, Toussaint had led a number of improvement initiatives as ThedaCare's chief medical officer. Performance would jump up after each one, only to slip back gradually to previous levels as staff members slowly reverted to old habits and new staff members, untrained in the improved methods, were hired. He believed that the reason for this pattern was the lack of a systematic approach for assuring that improvements went deep, took hold permanently, and could be cumulatively built upon.

At that time, ThedaCare operated like most health care operations in the United States. Doctors told nurses and staff what to do, and the nurses and staff did what they were told. Everyone wanted to do what was best for their patients, of course, but the myriad of rules put in place by the hospital administration, industry accrediting bodies, insurance companies, and state and federal governments meant the patients' interests were often lost in the resulting bureaucratic rules and inefficiencies.

Toussaint believed a new way of working was needed—one that actively involved employees on the front lines in creating better processes. While he wasn't aware of any health care organization in the United States that worked this way, he did know of a local snow-blower manufacturer, Ariens, Inc., that did. So he led a small team of ThedaCare managers on a benchmarking trip to Brillion, Wisconsin. There the managers had an epiphany. The manufacturer, by following the lean philosophy of employee-driven continuous improvement, had developed better systems to assure the error-free production of snow blowers than the systems ThedaCare used to avoid mistakes when dealing with its patients. This convinced Toussaint and his team to try using lean principles in their health care context.

Traditional ways of thinking about how patient care should be provided had to be overturned. In 2007, for example, ThedaCare began testing a "Collaborative Care" approach to delivering patient care in one of its hospitals. Instead of the traditional siloed and hierarchical approach, doctors, nurses, and pharmacists worked with patients as integrated teams. The teams made morning rounds together, and together developed the best care plan for each patient. The improvements in clinical results were dramatic. For example: medication defects per chart dropped from 1.05 (low by industry standards at the time) to 0.01, patient satisfaction rose from 68 to 90 percent, the average length of a hospital stay dropped 20 percent, and the average cost per case was reduced by 21 percent. The cost savings from Collaborative Care alone paid for an entirely new hospital tower designed specifically for that model of care.

ThedaCare also started extensive use of value stream mapping—a type of detailed flowcharting that helps identify problems, delays, and improvement opportunities—which it used to dramatically improve its performance in key areas. For example, as a result of a series of projects in the cardiac surgery area over a seven-year period, the number of deaths as a result of bypass surgery dropped from 4 percent of cases to almost zero, the cost of surgery was cut by 22 percent, and the average patient hospital stay dropped from 6.3 days to 4.9. These improvements also saved Theda-Care more than $27 million per year.

Although the major improvement projects did deliver significant results, Toussaint estimated that they accounted for only about 20 percent of ThedaCare's overall performance gains. The other 80 percent came from front-line ideas. Every front-line team holds a daily "huddle" in front of its idea board. The team discusses any new ideas and any issues with patients that arose during the morning rounds, reviews progress on existing ideas and improvement projects, assigns new actions to its members, and celebrates implemented ideas.

ThedaCare uses a hierarchy of problem-solving methods and tools. Problems that can be resolved with simple-to-implement ideas are moved from the raw ideas area of the board to the "just-do-it" area, assigned to a team member, and quickly implemented. More complex problems are moved to a different area of the board and managed as larger projects using the lean A3 improvement process. The progress of these projects is monitored as a regular part of the huddle process.

For even bigger problems, ThedaCare uses four-and-a-half day "rapid improvement events" (RIEs), another lean improvement methodology, sometimes referred to as *kaizen* events or *kaizen* blitzes. The typical RIE team consists of a mixture of front-line and management staff in the area being improved, a couple of members from other areas in order to bring different perspectives, and someone who represents the patients' perspective. This last member is often an actual patient.

Becoming idea driven was not easy for ThedaCare. Performance in several key areas actually declined before it began to improve, and a number of doctors and managers quit or had to be replaced along the way. A great deal of care was taken to instill an idea-driven culture; and to assure it would be sustained. Twice weekly, ThedaCare's senior managers meet in the "war room" to review performance. Unlike typical executive conference rooms, which are luxuriously furnished and formal, the war room is functionally furnished and its walls are festooned with tracking charts, data, and projects. One wall displays metrics that are reviewed at each meeting, a second wall has metrics that are reviewed weekly, a third is for monthly metrics, and the last is for quarterly and annual results.

This regular review of aggregated data does not, in and of itself, differentiate ThedaCare from other well-managed organizations. What is different is that every ThedaCare senior executive is required to spend time every week on the front lines checking into what is driving all of these numbers, assuring that the improvement processes at lower levels are working smoothly, and providing any needed coaching and support. As we mentioned in Chapter 2, even the CEO spends two hours each week on the front lines.

On a rotating basis, members of the senior leadership team also attend the weekly report-out sessions for the RIE teams. On Friday mornings, all teams that completed their RIE projects in the previous week come together to share their results at a large off-site gathering. Typically four or five RIE teams report on their projects and answer questions from the audience. Every presenting team is publicly thanked and roundly applauded.

While anyone in the company can attend these gatherings (and many do), new employees are required to attend.

To support all the front-line team improvement projects, ThedaCare has created a dedicated group of twenty "facilitators" trained in process improvement and lean tools. Employees volunteer for these two-year full-time positions both to gain valuable process improvement skills and to increase their chances of promotion. Roughly a third of ThedaCare's 150 highest-ranking managers are former facilitators.

With everyone in the organization involved with improvement ideas, ThedaCare has been able to innovate in the overall delivery of health care—an area where most health care organizations continue to struggle. It has been able to reduce costs substantially while improving clinical outcomes and patient satisfaction significantly.

CONCLUSION

Building an idea-driven organization is not easy, and it does not happen overnight. Time is needed to excise command-and-control thinking, to develop new habits and skills, and to create the management systems that promote rapid ongoing improvement and innovation.

Idea-driven organizations are relatively rare today, but we believe that twenty years from now they will be commonplace. All over the world, fundamental macroeconomic forces—such as globalization, rapid economic growth in developing nations, and the rise of the Internet—are forcing organizations of all kinds to do much more with much less, and to dramatically increase the rate at which they innovate and improve.

At the same time, the number of idea-driven organizations is increasing rapidly, and they are thriving in this new reality. Their broad-based success proves the superiority of the new management model and provides role models for others to learn from that did not exist just a few years ago.

In 1991, we published an article in *Sloan Management Review,* in which we pointed out that it was almost impossible to find effective idea systems in the United States. The ones we wrote about in that article were all in Japan, and all followed essentially the same *kaizen teian* process described in Chapter 5. By 2004, when we published *Ideas Are Free,* a handful of companies with high-performing idea systems could be found in North America, Europe, and various countries in Asia. There was a considerable variety in the approaches being used, and some of the systems were becoming quite sophisticated.

Today, there are quite a few organizations with mature high-performing idea systems, and they are capable of innovating at extraordinary rates. And we observe a rising interest in high-performing idea systems in government, health care, and education, sectors that are coming under great pressure to do more with less.

The adoption of high-performance idea systems by organizations over the last quarter century follows Gabriel Tarde's classic S-curve pattern of how an innovation or idea diffuses through a social system.[3] The acceptance of a new idea starts out slowly as it captures the interest of early adopters. As the new idea is refined and enhanced with ancillary ideas, and people learn more about how to use it to its best advantage, the rate of diffusion increases. Eventually, as the idea matures its diffusion gradually tapers off. Charted over time this adoption pattern looks like an S.

In his classic book *Diffusion of Innovations*, Everett Rogers identified five factors that determine the speed at which this pattern unfolds:[4]

- The *relative advantage* the new idea offers over existing thinking
- The idea's *compatibility* with current systems used by potential adopters
- How *complex* the new idea is to use
- How easy it is to try the new idea (*trialability*)
- The *observability* of the new idea and its advantages

On the one hand, a high-performance idea system confers a huge *relative advantage*. On the other hand, it is fairly *complex* and *difficult to try* precisely because it is so highly *incompatible* with the way that organizations have traditionally been run. This explains the relatively slow adoption of idea-driven principles to date.

But more and more leaders are realizing that they simply cannot produce the results they now need with the organizations they currently have. They are searching for solutions. At the same time, the growing number of high-performing systems around the world is increasing both their *observability* and the population of managers who understand the advantages of operating in an idea-driven manner. This growing base of experience and knowledge is making it ever easier for organizations to make the transformation.

We believe the evidence is clear. The idea-driven organization is an idea whose time has come!

KEY POINTS

✓ For the majority of leaders seeking to make their organizations more innovative, the first step should be to set up a high-performing idea system. There is a multifaceted interplay between innovation and front-line ideas, an interplay that most managers are not aware of. As a result, their organizations are far less innovative than they could be.

✓ The complexity and novelty of large innovations mean that many smaller ideas are required to get them to work effectively or sometimes even to work at all.

✓ Large numbers of small ideas create substantial new strategic capabilities that allow an organization to innovate in ways that would otherwise be impossible.

✓ Front-line ideas can transform routine innovations into major breakthroughs.

✓ Front-line ideas can directly open up new opportunities for innovation.

✓ Because most organizations are poorly aligned for ideas, their innovations require a great deal of championing. All this effort is usually accepted as the cost of innovating, and the underlying misalignments are never corrected, requiring future innovations to fight the same battles. But when organizations set up high-performing idea systems, they are forced to address their alignment problems, and this makes innovation much easier, too.

✓ Idea-driven organizations are relatively rare today, but we believe that twenty years from now they will be commonplace. All over the world, fundamental macroeconomic forces—such as globalization, rapid economic growth in developing nations, and the rise of the Internet—are forcing organizations of all kinds to do much more with much less, and to dramatically increase the rate at which they innovate and improve.

NOTES

CHAPTER 1

1. Six Sigma is a structured process improvement methodology, developed by Motorola and popularized by Jack Welch at GE, in which ad hoc improvement teams are overseen by specially trained individuals certified as "black belts," "green belts," and "yellow belts," who are responsible for assuring the problem-solving process follows prescribed protocols.

2. The story of Milliken's idea system is told in *Ideas Are Free*.

3. See F. A. Hayek, "The Use of Knowledge in Society," *American Economic Review* 35, no. 4 (September 1945): 519–530.

CHAPTER 2

1. Fred Luthans, "Successful vs. Effective Real Managers," *Academy of Management Executive* 2, no. 22 (1988): 127–132.

2. Peter Drucker shared this story with us during a series of personal discussions in 1990.

3. "Riverside County Debates Who Gets the Best Toilet Paper," *Los Angeles Times,* May 7, 2009.

4. A complete account of the experiment can be found in Philip Zimbardo, *The Lucifer Effect* (New York: Random House, 2008).

5. Ibid.

6. Adam Galinsky, Deborah Gruenfeld, and Joe Magee, "From Power to Action," *Journal of Personality and Social Psychology* 8, no. 3 (2003): 454.

7. "Military's Top Officers Face Review of Their Character," *New York Times,* April 13, 2013.

8. Jim Collins, *Good to Great: Why Some Companies Make the Leap and Others Don't* (New York: HarperCollins, 2001).

9. K. Benne and R. Chin, "Strategies of Change," in *The Planning of Change,* ed. W. Bennis, K. Benne, and R. Chin (New York: International Thompson Publishing, 1985).

10. We first encountered guided executive reading courses in Japan in the late 1980s, where they were being used by a number of leading companies to drive major transformational changes.

11. *Understanding Risk: Informing Decisions in a Democratic Society* (Washington, D.C.: National Research Council, 1996).

12. J. Dupuit, "De la mesure de l'utilité des travaux publics," *Annales des Pont et Chaussées 2,* no. 8 (1844): 332–375; an English translation was republished in *International Economic Papers* 2 (1952): 83–110.

CHAPTER 4

1. Frank B. Gilbreth, *Primer of Scientific Management* (New York: Van Nostrand, 1912), 68–69.

CHAPTER 8

1. World Health Organization, *The World Health Report* (Geneva: Author, 2000). This was the only year that WHO produced this report, as it was criticized for its methods and usefulness, particularly in the United States. Subsequent independent research largely confirmed its findings, at least with regard to the United States.

2. Cited in Steven Spears, *Chasing the Rabbit* (New York: McGraw-Hill, 2008).

3. Gabriel D. Tarde, *The Laws of Imitation* (New York: Holt, 1903).

4. Everett M. Rogers, *Diffusion of Innovations* (New York: Free Press, 1962).

ACKNOWLEDGMENTS

THIS BOOK WOULD NOT have come about without the help of a great many people.

First and foremost, we would like to thank the many front-line employees, managers, and senior leaders in the organizations we studied who gave so generously of their time and shared their information and stories so openly with us. A number of them deserve special mention: at Allianz China and Ayudhya Allianz, Wilf Blackburn (former CEO of both); at Alpha Natural Resources, Kevin Crutchfield (CEO), Rick McAlister (manager of Engineering Methods and Standards), and Randy McMillion (executive vice president of Business Excellence); at Brasilata, Antonio Texeira (CEO); at Big Y Foods, Donald D'Amour (CEO), Jack Henry (vice president of Employee Services), and Pat Shewchuk (manager of Employment Strategies and Inclusion); at the Clarion-Stockholm, Ulrika Bergstrom (Operations manager); at Coca-Cola Stockholm, Klas Bandmann (director of Continuous Improvement), Henrik Bennet (Strategic Planning manager), and Staffan Olsson (Operations Excellence manager); at Continental VDO, Gerhard Schadt (senior specialist, Coaching); at Graniterock, Bruce Woolpert (CEO); at HCSS, Mike Ryder (president) and Tom Webb (vice president); at Health New England, Peter Straley (CEO), Kim Kenney-Rockwal (director of HR), Jim Kessler (general counsel), and Joanne Walton-Bicknell (Business Improvement manager); at Hickory Chair, Jay Reardon (CEO); at the Maine Center for Disease Control, Dr. Sheila Pinette (director); at Pyromation, Pete Wilson (president) and Dan Atkinson (Operations manager); at Subaru Indiana Automotive, Tom

179

Easterday (executive vice president), Denise Coogan (manager of Safety and Environmental Compliance), and Matt Green (manager of Integrated Services for Heritage Integrative Services on-site at SIA); at Task Force Tips, Stewart McMillan (president); at ThedaCare, John Toussaint (former CEO); at the University of Southern Maine, Brynn Riley (project director); at Whirlpool, Nancy Tennant-Snyder (vice president of Core Competencies and Leadership) and Moises Norena (global director of Innovation).

Both our home institutions, the Isenberg School of Management at the University of Massachusetts and the College of Business at Valparaiso University, gave us strong support to write this book and have always been wonderful places to work.

Special thanks go to Louise Östberg, a Swedish friend and colleague, who helped us identify and work with a number of excellent companies. We are also indebted to Lars Nilsson at C2 Management for his openness and many introductions into leading Swedish companies.

The hardest part of our journey was writing the manuscript, which went through many drafts as we struggled to articulate our message. Gwen and J. Alan Robinson helped us immeasurably in this process, always challenging us to simplify and sharpen. We are also grateful to Michael Long, Scott Schenone, and J. D. Ward for their critical feedback on an early draft of the manuscript; to Lexie Schroeder for her counsel and creative work on our exhibits; and to Laura Larson, our highly talented copy editor.

We would never have been able to produce this book without the invaluable support of the incomparable team at Berrett-Koehler. Special thanks go to Neal Maillet, editorial director, for his steady encouragement, keen insights, and patient mentoring; to the Berrett-Koehler manuscript reviewers Wally Bock, Danielle Goodman, Jeffrey Kulick, and Lucie Newcomb; and to Michael Bass of Michael Bass Associates for his kind and rigorous shepherding of the manuscript through to final publication.

Finally, and most important, we will never be able to express the debt we owe our families, who were with us every step of the way and cheerfully endured our lengthy and numerous absences, and our camping in each other's houses for extended working visits. To our children Phoebe, Margot, Lexie, Liz, and Tori, and particularly our wives Margaret and Kate, we can only say: We could not have done it without you.

INDEX

ABOUT THE AUTHORS

Alan G. Robinson and Dean M. Schroeder are award-winning authors, consultants, and educators. They are the coauthors of the bestseller *Ideas Are Free: How the Idea Revolution Is Liberating People and Transforming Organizations*. Between them, they have advised hundreds of organizations in more than twenty-five countries around the world on how to improve their creativity, innovativeness, and overall performance.

Alan Robinson has authored or coauthored seven books and more than sixty articles. His book *Corporate Creativity,* coauthored with Sam Stern, was a finalist for the *Financial Times*/Booz Allen & Hamilton Global Best Business Book Award, and it was named "Book of the Year" by the Academy of Human Resource Management. He has a PhD from the Whiting School of Engineering at the Johns Hopkins University and a BA/MA in mathematics from the University of Cambridge. He teaches at the Isenberg School of Management at the University of Massachusetts at Amherst.

Karin Woodside

Dean M. Schroeder has authored or coauthored three books and more than eighty articles. He is the Herbert and Agnes Schulz Professor of Management at Valparaiso University in Indiana. He is a two-time Shingo Prize winner, and for five years he served on the board of the U.S. Malcolm Baldrige National Quality Award. He earned a PhD in strategic management from the Carlson School of Management at the University of Minnesota, and he has a BS in engineering from Minnesota and an MBA from the University of Montana.

For more about how to unlock the power in bottom-up ideas in your organization, visit the authors' website at www.idea-driven.com.

Also by Alan G. Robinson and Dean M. Schroeder

Ideas Are Free
How the Idea Revolution Is Liberating People and Transforming Organizations

A worker in one of Europe's largest wireless communication companies fixed an error in his company's billing software and saved some $26 million per year. A secretary at Grapevine Canyon Ranch proposed a simple change to the company's website that brought it to the top of search engine listings. A guard at the Massachusetts Department of Correction saved $56,000 a year by suggesting the use of digital cameras instead of film to process new inmates.

This was the first book in which Alan Robinson and Dean Schroeder described the power and promise of employee ideas. They draw on extensive research with more than 300 organizations around the world to show how managers can elicit and encourage groundbreaking ideas from frontline employees.

"This empowering book is a refreshingly simple examination of how corporate creativity can happen." —**Fast Company**

"Recommended for all business collections." —**Library Journal**

Paperback, 264 pages, ISBN 978-1-57675-374-3
PDF ebook, ISBN 978-1-60509-017-7

Berrett–Koehler Publishers, Inc.
www.bkconnection.com

800.929.2929

Berrett–Koehler
Publishers

Berrett-Koehler is an independent publisher dedicated to an ambitious mission: *Creating a World That Works for All*.

We believe that to truly create a better world, action is needed at all levels—individual, organizational, and societal. At the individual level, our publications help people align their lives with their values and with their aspirations for a better world. At the organizational level, our publications promote progressive leadership and management practices, socially responsible approaches to business, and humane and effective organizations. At the societal level, our publications advance social and economic justice, shared prosperity, sustainability, and new solutions to national and global issues.

A major theme of our publications is "Opening Up New Space." Berrett-Koehler titles challenge conventional thinking, introduce new ideas, and foster positive change. Their common quest is changing the underlying beliefs, mindsets, institutions, and structures that keep generating the same cycles of problems, no matter who our leaders are or what improvement programs we adopt.

We strive to practice what we preach—to operate our publishing company in line with the ideas in our books. At the core of our approach is stewardship, which we define as a deep sense of responsibility to administer the company for the benefit of all of our "stakeholder" groups: authors, customers, employees, investors, service providers, and the communities and environment around us.

We are grateful to the thousands of readers, authors, and other friends of the company who consider themselves to be part of the "BK Community." We hope that you, too, will join us in our mission.

A BK Business Book

This book is part of our BK Business series. BK Business titles pioneer new and progressive leadership and management practices in all types of public, private, and nonprofit organizations. They promote socially responsible approaches to business, innovative organizational change methods, and more humane and effective organizations.

Berrett–Koehler
Publishers

A community dedicated to creating
a world that works for all

Dear Reader,

Thank you for picking up this book and joining our worldwide community of Berrett-Koehler readers. We share ideas that bring positive change into people's lives, organizations, and society.

To welcome you, we'd like to offer you a free e-book. You can pick from among twelve of our bestselling books by entering the promotional code **BKP92E** here: http://www.bkconnection.com/welcome.

When you claim your free e-book, we'll also send you a copy of our e-newsletter, the *BK Communiqué*. Although you're free to unsubscribe, there are many benefits to sticking around. In every issue of our newsletter you'll find

- A free e-book
- Tips from famous authors
- Discounts on spotlight titles
- Hilarious insider publishing news
- A chance to win a prize for answering a riddle

Best of all, our readers tell us, "Your newsletter is the only one I actually read." So claim your gift today, and please stay in touch!

Sincerely,

Charlotte Ashlock
Steward of the BK Website

Questions? Comments? Contact me at bkcommunity@bkpub.com.

Certified

Corporation
bcorporation.net